SENSATIONAL SOUPS

SENSATIONAL SOUPS

JUDY KNIPE

FAWCETT COLUMBINE ◆ NEW YORK

A Fawcett Columbine Book
Published by Ballantine Books

Copyright © 1994 by Judy Knipe

Library of Congress Cataloging-in-Publication Data

Knipe, Judy.
Sensational soups / Judy Knipe.
p.   cm.
Includes index.
ISBN 0-449-90672-8
1. Soups.   I. Title.
TX757.K59   1994
641.8'13—dc20   93-38297
CIP

BOOK DESIGN BY BARBARA MARKS
Illustrations by Patti Hefner
Cover design by Kristine V. Mills
Cover photo by George Kerrigan

Manufactured in the United States of America

First Edition: January 1994

10 9 8 7 6 5 4 3 2 1

For Pam Marron, who ate up all the good soup,

and

in memory of my grandmother, Sonya Rutberg, who every
Friday night would say, as she served that great chicken
soup, "Children, this is the best one I ever made."

ACKNOWLEDGMENTS

Thanks first to my editor, Ginny Faber, for her encouragement, advice, and patience, and to Carla Glasser, my agent and the party whip. For recipes and generous time, tastings, and love: Linda Amster; Toni Burbank and Tony Koltz; Rosemarie, Marisa, and Giancarlo Garipoli; Janet Gilbert; Ethel and Paul Hultberg; Charles Kaiser; my sister, Betty Kohlenberg; Barbara Marks; Richard Meislin; Syd, Brad, Bobby, and Jonathan Miner; Jackie Montgomery and Alan Luks; Hendrik Uyttendale; Ted Whittemore; and special thanks to my aunt, Tesse Kosoff, who doesn't even like soup and had to eat an awful lot of it.

Contents

INTRODUCTION

. . . .

Soup is a universal means of satisfying our deep human need for sustenance and good flavor, and few foods are more gratifying, nourishing, or comforting.

That's just the beginning. Soups offer extraordinary value for the money, since the ingredients in most are reasonably priced and available year round. Soups require almost no culinary skill, no elaborate equipment, and most of them taste better prepared in advance. Soups store well, and the majority can be reheated with no loss of flavor or texture. Soups are versatile, serving as starters, main courses, and desserts. Soup can be a clear, shimmering consommé with a few carved vegetables floating at the bottom or it can be as thick and hearty as minestrone.

About half the recipes in this book are primarily for vegetable (although not necessarily vegetarian) soups. Variations are suggested in many cases, but since soup-making is a spontaneous activity, depending on the occasion, the ingredients available, and your inclinations, experiment by substituting, adding, and subtracting ingredients. And, because most of the ingredients are so simple, use the best quality you can find.

Although the soups in this book can be used as starters, most of them, even the lighter soups, are intended as main course meals to be served with bread, salad, and a fruit dessert. These are the soups I serve my friends and family, and I hope you will do the same.

SENSATIONAL SOUPS

STOCKS

Stock is a liquid whose principal flavor—chicken, beef, fish, vegetables—is enhanced by aromatic vegetables, herbs, and spices. Stocks are the essence of soup-making, and while homemade stocks are not necessarily more economical than those that are canned or derived from powders and bouillon cubes, they pay off lavishly in flavor.

With this said, I believe that, for the home cook, making stock on a regular basis is either a pleasurable pursuit or a tedious chore. If you enjoy stock-making, the actual work involved is negligible, the aroma that fills the kitchen while the stock is cooking is comforting and homey, and the stock itself is the ultimate reward. Furthermore, one bout of stock-making can produce enough for more than one soup recipe. Stocks freeze beautifully, and you can cash in later.

Still, if you don't like making stock, you probably won't do it. Fortunately, there are commercial products that are fair, although never perfect, substitutes for homemade stock. Among these are chicken and beef broths and stocks that can be used direct from the can, canned condensed broths that are diluted, bouillon cubes, and powders. All of these products have flavor enhancers and preservatives, at the very least. I suggest you experiment with whatever varieties and brands are available to you and then choose what best suits your palate and pocketbook. The recipes in this book use canned condensed chicken and beef broth, diluted with more water than is called for on the label instructions to help minimize their canned taste. If you feel inclined, you can greatly improve a canned broth by simmering it for a few minutes with some chopped carrot and onion, some fresh or dried herbs congenial to the soup you'll be making, and a pinch of brown sugar. Strain before using.

Bottled clam juice is the only commercial substitute for homemade fish stock. However, many fishmongers make and freeze their own stock, which is far tastier than the clam juice.

Canned vegetable broths and vegetable bouillon cubes usually have a persistent aftertaste and are so awful that you are better off using water.

Here's what you need to know about making stock:

EQUIPMENT

Almost no special equipment is required for making stock. Strainers, colanders, and bowls are found in every standard kitchen. Aside from that, you will need:

A stock pot—a tall stainless steel or other nonreactive metal 12- to 16-quart pot with a cover.

A stainless steel mesh skimmer, which, although not strictly necessary, is nice to have for removing the foam and other impurities that rise to the surface of the stock during cooking. However, a large long-handled spoon will do just as well.

Freezer containers in pint and quart sizes for storing the stock.

MAKING STOCK

Once you've assembled your ingredients and start to cook, there are several procedures specific to producing a good stock.

Skimming: With a large spoon or the skimmer, remove the foam and scum that rise to the surface, especially at the onset of cooking. These impurities, if not skimmed off, will cloud the color and impair the flavor of the stock. Most of the scum can be removed during the first 5 minutes of cooking, with an occasional skimming at intervals later on.

Reducing stocks: If your finished stock is to be the basis of a soup with very flavorful ingredients, there's no need to reduce it. However, if it must stand more or less on its own merits, as in a lightly embellished consommé, or in matzoh ball soup, for example, you can intensify its flavor by reducing it: Simply boil gently until the stock reduces by about a third, tasting occasionally, until it is very savory. You can reduce stock before or after freezing; one advantage of doing it before is that it takes up less freezer space.

Cooling and degreasing the stock: Strain the finished stock into a bowl and allow it to cool, uncovered, at room temperature. Cover the bowl with plastic wrap and chill the stock until any fat that has not been skimmed off during cooking congeals on the surface. Remove the fat with a spatula, a skimmer, or a spoon.

Storage: Pour the stock into storage containers with tight lids and refrigerate for 2 to 3 days or freeze for up to 2 months, except as noted in individual recipes. I store stock for soups in pint- and quart-sized containers. If you plan to defrost stock in a microwave oven, use storage vessels that are microwavable.

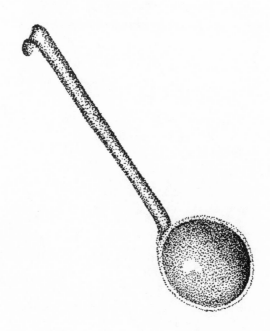

BROWN BEEF STOCK

. . . .

MAKES A GENEROUS 3 QUARTS

Rich beef stock is the basis for Creamed Pear and Onion Soup (page 100), French Onion Soup (page 96), and other soups made primarily from vegetables. When cooked beef is an important ingredient in the soup, as in Hearty Beef and Vegetable Soup (page 33) and Beef and Cabbage Soup (page 32), make the stock using boneless chuck or brisket as part of the meat-and-bone combination. The meat will retain enough of its flavor, even after 5 hours of cooking, to taste good in the soup.

◆

4 pounds meaty raw beef bones, sawed into 2-inches pieces, or 2 pounds lean boneless chuck roast and 2 pounds beef marrow bones

2 large carrots, peeled and cut into chunks

2 large onions, peeled and quartered

2 medium leeks, trimmed, halved lengthwise, and well washed

2 celery ribs, trimmed and cut into chunks

5 quarts cold water

2 large garlic cloves, peeled and crushed with the flat of a knife

1 large tomato, cored and coarsely chopped, 1 tablespoon good-quality tomato paste, or 3 sun-dried tomatoes

6 to 8 sprigs Italian parsley

3 or 4 sprigs fresh oregano or thyme

1 large bay leaf

6 or 7 allspice berries, or 4 or 5 whole cloves

½ teaspoon black peppercorns

Salt

Preheat the oven to 450°F.

Spread out the beef bones in a large, shallow roasting pan and roast them until they are richly browned, 35 to 40 minutes, turning them after 20 minutes. Transfer the bones to a 10- to 12-quart stock pot and set aside.

Drain most of the fat from the baking pan, add the carrots, onions, leeks, and celery and roast them, stirring occasionally, for about 20 minutes, or until they are lightly browned. Transfer the vegetables to the stock pot.

Add 2 cups of the water to the roasting pan and deglaze over direct heat, scraping up all the caramelized bits of meat and vegetable. Pour the deglazing liquid into the stock pot, add the garlic, tomato, parsley, oregano, bay leaf, allspice berries, and peppercorns, then add enough cold water to cover all the ingredients generously, about 4½ quarts. Bring the stock to a simmer over moderate heat, skimming off all the foam as it rises to the surface. After the stock has simmered for about 5 minutes, cover the pot loosely, lower the heat, and simmer very gently for 5 hours, skimming every now and then and adding more water as needed to keep the ingredients covered. During the last 30 minutes of cooking, add salt to taste, using a moderate hand, especially if the stock will be reduced further.

Strain the stock into a bowl and allow it to cool to room temperature. Refrigerate for at least 5 hours or overnight, then skim off the fat that has congealed on the surface.

BROWN BEEF AND OXTAIL STOCK

For an even richer stock, instead of all beef, use 1½ to 2 pounds oxtails and 2 to 2½ pounds beef shin. Brown the meats and cook as directed. After 2 hours of cooking, remove the oxtail, strip off the meat and reserve it for another recipe (Beef and Cabbage Soup, page 32, for instance), and return the bones to the soup kettle. Continue cooking as directed.

Pork Stock

Pork stock—rich, flavorful, and very easy to make—is the basis for Pozole (page 40) and Pork and Cabbage Soup (page 38), and it can also be used to enrich vegetable and bean soups. Unless you plan to use the cooked pork in your soup or in another dish, ask your butcher for bones that have been removed from pork loins or shoulders. When these are not available, buy the cheapest cut of pork you can. Although the pork itself may be quite fatty, especially the less expensive cuts, the pork fat congeals after refrigeration into a solid "platter" that can be lifted quite conveniently from the surface of the stock.

◆

3 pounds fresh pork, mostly bones
1 to 4 garlic cloves, peeled and crushed with the flat of a knife
2 or 3 fresh sage leaves
1 sprig fresh rosemary or ½ teaspoon dried rosemary
2 sprigs Italian parsley
1 bay leaf
3 quarts water
4 black peppercorns
Salt

Combine the pork, garlic, sage, rosemary, parsley, bay leaf, water, and peppercorns in a 5-quart saucepan and bring to a boil over high heat. Cover the pan, reduce the heat, and simmer the stock, partially covered, for 1 hour.

If you intend to use the pork meat for a soup or another dish, remove it from the stock, strip the meat from the bones and reserve it, and return the bones to the stock. Simmer 1 hour longer. If the stock is intended as the base for a bean soup, do not add salt. Otherwise, add a moderate amount of salt and simmer 5 minutes longer.

Strain the stock into a bowl and allow it to cool to room temperature. Refrigerate for at least 5 hours or overnight, then skim off the fat that has congealed on the surface. Use at once or store as directed in refrigerator or freezer.

TURKEY STOCK

For some of us, the best reason for roasting a whole turkey is having that enormous carcass left over for making stock. *Never* throw out anything from your turkey. Save the carcass, any bones left from the wings, legs, and thighs, all the skin, even leftover gravy. All can be frozen for months or cooked up right away. Turkey stock, more robust than chicken, is great for hearty soups and stews.

♦

1 carcass from a 17- to 20-pound roast turkey

Leftover turkey gravy (optional)

2 medium-large onions, peeled and halved

2 large garlic cloves, peeled and gently crushed with the flat of a knife

2 large or 3 medium carrots, peeled and cut into chunks

1 large parsnip, peeled and cut into chunks

3 celery ribs with leaves, root ends trimmed, cut into chunks

1 or 2 medium leeks, root ends and all but 1 inch of greens trimmed, halved, cut into chunks, and rinsed under running water

5 quarts water

5 sprigs dill

5 sprigs Italian parsley

2 bay leaves

4 or 5 whole cloves

½ teaspoon black peppercorns

Salt

Combine the turkey, gravy (if using), onions, garlic, carrots, parsnip, celery, leeks, water, dill, parsley, bay leaves, cloves, and peppercorns in a 12-quart stock pot and bring to a boil over high heat. Lower the heat and skim the foam from the surface for about 5 minutes.

Partially cover the pot, leaving just a sliver of space between the lid and the rim of the pot, and simmer the stock very slowly for 4 hours, adding enough water to keep the ingredients covered and skimming occasionally. Salt the stock very lightly during the last 15 minutes of cooking.

(continued)

Strain the stock into a bowl and allow it to cool to room temperature, then refrigerate for at least 4 hours or overnight. Remove the fat that has congealed on the surface and transfer the stock to storage containers. (The chilled stock will be gelatinous; you can reheat it gently for easier transfer to containers.)

CHICKEN STOCK

MAKES A GENEROUS 3 QUARTS

Chicken stock is incredibly versatile. In addition to its use as a soup base, it goes into stews and sauces, makes sublime risottos, and is vastly superior to water as the cooking liquid for bulgur, couscous, barley, and other grains. Freeze it in assorted quantities—you'll revel in your foresightedness later on. This recipe produces a very intense stock. For a lighter version, add an additional 4 cups of water.

♦

4 pounds chicken parts, preferably wings

5 quarts water

2 medium onions (9 to 10 ounces total), peeled and halved

2 large garlic cloves, peeled and gently crushed with the flat of a knife

2 large or 3 medium carrots (about 7 ounces), peeled and cut into chunks

1 large parsnip (about 4 ounces), peeled and cut into chunks

3 celery ribs with leaves, root ends trimmed, cut into chunks

2 medium leeks, root ends and all but 1 inch of greens trimmed, halved, well washed, and cut into chunks

5 to 10 sprigs dill

5 to 10 sprigs Italian parsley

2 bay leaves

½ teaspoon black peppercorns

4 or 5 whole cloves

Salt

Rinse off the chicken parts under cold running water and place in a 10-quart stock pot. Add 3½ quarts of the water and bring the mixture to a simmer, but not a rolling boil, over moderate heat. Let the stock simmer for about 10 minutes, skimming off the foam and impurities as they rise to the surface.

Meanwhile, prepare the onions, garlic, carrots, parsnip, celery, and leeks. Place the leeks in a strainer and wash under lukewarm running water, rubbing off all the sand clinging to the green parts.

When the stock is perfectly clear, add the vegetables and enough water to cover them—1 to 1½ quarts. Bring the stock back to a simmer and cook for about 5 minutes, skimming off the foam. Add the dill, parsley, bay leaves, peppercorns, and cloves. Partially cover the pot and simmer the stock very slowly for 5 hours, skimming occasionally. (For a less rich stock, add water from time to time to keep the ingredients covered.)

Strain the stock into a bowl and allow it to cool to room temperature, then refrigerate for at least 4 hours or overnight. Remove the fat that has congealed on the surface and transfer the stock to storage containers.

CHICKEN STOCK FROM CARCASSES

For people like me, who feel compelled to freeze poultry carcasses, or who deglaze roasting pans and save the drippings; for those who can't discard that last ¼ cup of turkey gravy; and for those who know the day of reckoning when they see it (the freezer looks like a graveyard), there is the satisfaction of doing yourself a double favor: You can clean out your freezer and make a really inexpensive stock at

(continued)

the same time. Use 4 pounds of any combination of chicken carcasses, chicken bones that you have accumulated in a freezer bag (wing tips, backs, breast bones, necks), and fresh chicken parts. Add leftover drippings and gravy as well and cook as directed in the master recipe. (You won't get a clear stock if you use gravy in it, but the flavor will be terrific.)

TARRAGON CHICKEN STOCK

Thirty minutes before the end of cooking, add 5 or 6 sprigs of fresh tarragon to the stock. Since tarragon is an assertive herb, use this version judiciously (the Carrot Tarragon soup on page 86 is an example).

SMOKED CHICKEN STOCK

Use 1 smoked chicken carcass and 3 unsmoked carcasses, or enough smoked chicken parts to equal 4 pounds, and cook as directed. The result is a delicious stock with a subtle, smoky flavor. Use the stock as the base for a wild mushroom risotto or for bean soups.

FISH STOCK

MAKES 2 QUARTS

STORAGE
In the refrigerator for 1 day; frozen for up to 2 months

Fish stock is not only very easy to make, it is exceptionally cheap, since many fishmongers will provide fish heads and carcasses without charge. Bottled clam juice that has been doctored with onion, carrot, celery, and fresh herbs is an acceptable substitute for homemade fish stock. (If you find it too salty, add a peeled, diced potato to the other vegetables.) This recipe makes a light, flavorful stock that can be further reduced for a more concentrated broth.

◆

2½ to 3 pounds fish heads, carcasses, and skin from nonoily white fish, rinsed and drained

1 large onion, peeled and chopped

2 carrots, peeled and sliced

2 celery ribs, sliced

3 quarts cold water

1 bay leaf

2 or 3 thyme sprigs

2 or 3 Italian parsley sprigs

6 black peppercorns

Salt

In a 6-quart stainless steel or other nonreactive stock pot or saucepan, combine the fish, onion, carrots, celery, water, bay leaf, thyme, parsley, peppercorns, and a moderate amount of salt. Bring the stock to a boil over high heat, reduce the heat, and cook at a slow boil, uncovered, for 20 to 25 minutes, skimming the foam as it rises to the top.

Strain the stock through a colander lined with a double layer of cheesecloth and allow to cool before storing in the refrigerator.

TOMATO FISH STOCK

STORAGE
In the refrigerator for 1 day;
frozen for up to 2 months

Shallots, leek, fennel, white
wine, and tomatoes add a
subtle flavor to this stock, which is
an excellent base for fish and
shellfish stews.

◆

2½ to 3 pounds fish heads, trimmings, and bones, rinsed under
    cold running water and drained
2 large shallots, peeled and minced
3 garlic cloves, peeled and minced
1 medium leek, white part only, trimmed, quartered, sliced,
    and rinsed
½ fennel bulb, trimmed, cored, and sliced (optional)
1 carrot, peeled and sliced
1 celery rib, trimmed and sliced
1 cup canned imported plum tomatoes, drained and crushed
1 cup dry white wine
3 quarts cold water
1 bay leaf
2 strips lemon zest
2 or 3 thyme sprigs
2 or 3 Italian parsley sprigs
6 peppercorns
Salt

In a large stainless steel or enameled saucepan, combine the
fish, shallots, garlic, leek, fennel (if desired), carrot, celery,
tomatoes, wine, water, bay leaf, lemon zest, thyme, parsley,
and peppercorns. Add a moderate amount of salt and bring
the stock to a boil over high heat. Reduce the heat and
simmer the stock for 20 to 25 minutes, skimming off the
foam as it rises to the surface.

Strain the stock through a colander lined with cheesecloth,
cool, and refrigerate. For a more intense flavor, reduce the
strained stock by about a third by cooking over high heat.

POTATO SOUP BASE

This thickened stock is a versatile base that can be tailored to suit the other ingredients in your soup. It can be made with poultry, meat, fish, or vegetable stock, or vegetable cooking water as part of the liquid, or you can use all water. Fat rendered from salt pork or pancetta will add flavor to fish and vegetable chowders. Made with olive oil, extra garlic, and perhaps a leek, and the cooking liquid from dried beans, the base is a delicious foundation for bean and other vegetable soups. For curried soups, add the curry powder to the sautéed onion and garlic and cook a few minutes longer.

♦

1 tablespoon butter, olive oil, vegetable oil, or other fat

1 large onion, peeled and chopped

1 to 4 garlic cloves, peeled and minced

6 to 8 ounces Red Bliss, new, all-purpose, Yukon Gold, or other potatoes, cut into ½-inch cubes

1 quart Roasted Vegetable Stock (page 18), Bean Stock (page 19), Chicken Stock (page 12), Brown Beef Stock (page 8), or one 10½-ounce can concentrated chicken or beef broth plus enough water to equal 1 quart

1 sprig fresh rosemary, 3 sprigs fresh thyme, or 1 pinch dried thyme

Salt

Freshly ground black pepper

Combine the fat, onion, and garlic in a heavy 2- to 2½-quart saucepan, place over moderate heat, and sauté for 5 minutes. Add the potatoes, stock, herb, and salt and pepper to taste and bring to a boil over high heat. Lower the heat and simmer the soup base, covered, for 15 minutes, or until the potatoes are tender.

Remove the herb sprig(s) and purée the soup base in a food processor fitted with the steel blade. It is now ready to use.

ROASTED VEGETABLE STOCK

MAKES 5 CUPS

Rich and full-bodied, this stock can be used interchangeably with chicken stock in most vegetable soup recipes. Instead of water, use the steaming or cooking liquid from vegetables whose flavor is not overpowering, such as carrots, green peas, green beans, and asparagus—no broccoli, brussels sprouts, cabbage, or cauliflower.

◆

2 medium onions, peeled and thickly sliced
2 or 3 garlic cloves, peeled and gently crushed with the flat of a
    knife and peeled
1 large leek, white only and 1 inch of green, trimmed, split
    lengthwise, thickly sliced, and well rinsed
2 shallots, peeled and halved
2 parsnips, peeled and thickly sliced
2 carrots, peeled and thickly sliced
2 celery stalks, trimmed and thickly sliced
2 tablespoons vegetable oil
2 quarts water
2 or 3 sprigs Italian parsley
2 or 3 sprigs fresh thyme
1 sprig fresh rosemary
1 bay leaf
6 to 10 black peppercorns
Salt

Preheat the oven to 450° F.

Combine the onions, garlic, leek, shallots, parsnips, carrots, and celery in a large shallow flameproof roasting pan. Drizzle the oil over the vegetables, then toss them to coat with the oil. Spread the vegetables evenly in the pan and roast them for 30 minutes, stirring 3 times so that they brown evenly.

Scrape the vegetables into a 3-quart saucepan. Pour 1 cup of the water into the roasting pan and deglaze over direct heat, stirring up all the browned bits of vegetable with a wooden spoon or a spatula. Pour the deglazing liquid over the vegetables, add the remaining water, the parsley, thyme, rosemary, bay leaf, and peppercorns, and bring to a boil over high heat. Reduce the heat and simmer the stock for 40 minutes, partially covered. Add salt to taste during the last 5 minutes of cooking.

Strain the stock into a bowl, pressing on the vegetables with the back of a ladle to extract as much of the liquid as possible. Cool before storing in the refrigerator.

BEAN STOCK

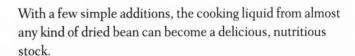

STORAGE
In the refrigerator for 2 to 3 days; frozen for up to 2 months

With a few simple additions, the cooking liquid from almost any kind of dried bean can become a delicious, nutritious stock.

Place the soaked, rinsed dried beans in a saucepan and add cold water to cover by 2 inches, then add an extra quart or more of water, a whole, peeled onion stuck with a clove, a bay leaf, and sprigs of fresh herbs such as parsley, thyme, or rosemary. Cook the beans until they are tender, add a moderate amount of salt to taste, and cook 5 to 10 minutes longer.

Drain the beans and discard the onion, bay leaf, and herbs. Reserve the cooking water and cool and store the liquid and beans separately. You should use the beans in a day or two— they don't freeze well by themselves—but the stock can be frozen for future soups.

FISH, MEAT, AND POULTRY SOUPS

W ith the exception of Shrimp Soup with Saffron and Tomatoes (page 30), these are hearty soups meant to be served as one-course meals. Most of them can be prepared in advance and cooked in less than an hour, so are ideal for busy cooks. Except as noted, these soups may be stored in the refrigerator for a day or two, or frozen for up to 2 months. Remember that freezing tends to blunt the edge of herbs and spices. When you reheat a previously frozen soup, taste carefully; you may need to add seasonings to freshen and punch up the flavor.

MUSSEL SOUP 23

BARBARA'S FISH SOUP (COTRIADE) 24

CLAM CHOWDER I 26

CLAM CHOWDER II 28

SHRIMP SOUP WITH SAFFRON AND TOMATOES 30

BEEF AND CABBAGE SOUP 32

HEARTY BEEF AND VEGETABLE SOUP 33

BEEF AND CABBAGE BORSCHT 34

RUTH'S RATATOUILLE SOUP WITH MEATBALLS 36

PORK AND CABBAGE SOUP 38

POZOLE 40

MATZOH BALL SOUP 42

CHICKEN NOODLE SOUP WITH VEGETABLES 44

CURRIED CREAM OF CHICKEN SOUP WITH APPLES AND ONIONS 46

TURKEY AND BARLEY SOUP 47

TURKEY, WILD RICE, AND VEGETABLE SOUP 48

MUSSEL SOUP

. . . .

SERVES 4

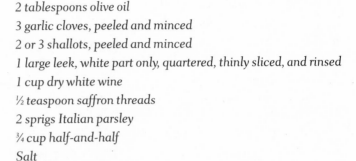

Farmed mussels, which need only debearding and a good rinse, are delicious in this creamy version of moules marinières, made with a pinch of saffron for added richness. The soup cooks in less than 20 minutes, and should be served at once, not stored. Serve with the wine used to make the soup, Italian or French bread toasts to soak up the creamy broth, and follow with a salad.

♦

2 tablespoons olive oil
3 garlic cloves, peeled and minced
2 or 3 shallots, peeled and minced
1 large leek, white part only, quartered, thinly sliced, and rinsed
1 cup dry white wine
½ teaspoon saffron threads
2 sprigs Italian parsley
¾ cup half-and-half
Salt
Freshly ground pepper
3 pounds mussels, scrubbed, debearded, and rinsed

In a flameproof 5-quart casserole, combine the olive oil, garlic, shallots, and leek and cook over moderate heat for 4 or 5 minutes. Do not allow the vegetables to brown. Add the wine, saffron, and parsley, and continue cooking, uncovered, over moderate heat for about 5 minutes, or until the wine is reduced to about ¼ cup. Add the half-and-half and cook for about 3 minutes, uncovered, or until the cream is partially reduced. Add salt to taste. Add the mussels, cover the casserole, and cook over high heat for 4 to 5 minutes, or until all the mussels are open. Remove the parsley sprigs and serve at once from the casserole.

BARBARA'S FISH SOUP (COTRIADE)

Part of the charm of this soup is its simplicity, and I prefer to make it with only one fish—scrod, haddock, or halibut, for instance—that is flavorful but not overwhelming. It's a lovely one-course meal served with a crisp white wine, garlic bread, and salad.

◆

2 medium potatoes, peeled, halved, and sliced
3 carrots, peeled and sliced
1 fennel bulb, trimmed, quartered, cored, and sliced
1 medium onion, peeled, quartered, and sliced
1 leek, white part only, quartered lengthwise, sliced, and rinsed
5 to 10 garlic cloves, peeled and halved
Salt
Freshly ground black pepper
2 sprigs Italian parsley
2 or 3 sprigs fresh thyme, or a pinch of dried thyme
¼ cup olive oil
Approximately 5 cups water or Fish Stock (page 15)
1 to 1¼ pounds firm white fish fillets (scrod, haddock, snapper, halibut) cut into 1-inch pieces
Rouille (page 121)

Layer the vegetables in a heavy 4-quart saucepan, starting with the potatoes, and sprinkle each layer sparingly with salt and pepper. Bury the parsley and thyme among the vegetables, then drizzle the olive oil over the top. Add enough cold water or fish stock to barely cover the top of the vegetables. Cover the pan and bring the soup to a boil over high heat. Reduce the heat and cook the soup at a slow boil until the vegetables are tender, about 30 minutes.

Remove the parsley and thyme sprigs. Arrange the fish on top of the vegetables, cover the pan, and cook at a boil until the fish just begins to flake, 3 or 4 minutes. Serve at once with the rouille.

SHELLFISH SOUP

Add 3 fresh plum tomatoes, shredded, or 3 drained canned plum tomatoes, crushed, to the vegetables, and put in a strip of orange zest with the herbs. For a more luxurious flavor, use Tomato Fish Stock (page 16) instead of water. Cook the vegetables as directed for about 30 minutes. Remove the herbs and orange zest. Add scrubbed mussels and clams, shelled shrimp, sea scallops, and/or rings of squid to the soup along with or instead of the fish fillets. Cover and cook until the mussels and clams have opened, and serve at once.

CLAM CHOWDER I

Ounce for ounce of meat, cherrystone and little neck clams cost more than lobster, which means that chowder made from fresh clams is becoming a luxury item. Still, the fresh clams are delicious, especially in this classic recipe. The chowder tastes best made a day in advance.

◆

2 to 3 pounds cherrystone clams, scrubbed

1 cup water

2⅓ to 3 ounces rindless salt pork, cut into ¼-inch dice

2 tablespoons plus 1 teaspoon unsalted butter

1 medium onion, peeled and chopped

1 celery rib, trimmed, halved lengthwise, and thinly sliced

2 cups peeled diced potatoes

Salt

Freshly ground black pepper

1½ tablespoons flour

2 cups milk

Drops of Worcestershire sauce

Combine the clams and water in a large heavy saucepan, cover, and steam over high heat until the clams open. Remove the clams from the pan, discard the shells, and reserve the clam meat, covered. Pour the clam broth through a strainer lined with a paper towel and add enough water to equal 2 cups. Refrigerate.

In a heavy 2½- to 3-quart saucepan, cook the salt pork over moderate heat until the fat is rendered and the pork is browned. Watch carefully toward the end of cooking to see that the pork doesn't burn. With a slotted spoon, transfer the pork to drain on a double layer of paper towels.

Pour out all but 2 teaspoons of fat from the saucepan and return the pan to the heat. Add 1 teaspoon of butter and the onion and sauté for 3 minutes. Add the celery and sauté 2 minutes longer. Add the drained salt pork, potatoes, reserved clam broth, and salt and pepper to taste, and bring the soup to a boil. Reduce the heat and simmer the potatoes, covered, for about 15 minutes, or until they are just tender.

Meanwhile, melt the 2 tablespoons of butter in a 1-quart saucepan over moderately low heat. Sprinkle the flour into the pan and cook, stirring constantly, for 2 to 3 minutes, or until the flour is thoroughly absorbed and heated through. Slowly stir in the milk and cook, stirring often to prevent lumps, for about 5 minutes. Stir this white sauce into the potato mixture, add drops of Worcestershire sauce and salt and pepper to taste, and continue to simmer the soup, partially covered, for 10 minutes.

Chill the chowder mixture overnight. The next day, just before serving, bring the chowder back to a gentle simmer. Cut the clams into small pieces, stir them into the simmering chowder, and cook 3 or 4 minutes longer. Serve hot with soda crackers.

CLAM CHOWDER II

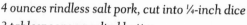

Frozen chopped quahogs or surf clams, which are carried by many fishmongers, are a more than adequate substitute for fresh clams in the shell. The clams are sold in 1-pound containers and can be defrosted overnight in the refrigerator. Like the preceding chowder, this develops flavor overnight, so make it a day ahead if possible.

◆

4 ounces rindless salt pork, cut into ¼-inch dice

3 tablespoons unsalted butter

1 medium onion, chopped

1 celery rib, trimmed, quartered lengthwise, and thinly sliced

3 to 4 cups peeled cubed potatoes

1 cup water

2 cups bottled clam juice

Salt

Freshly ground black pepper

1½ tablespoons flour

2 cups milk

1 pound frozen quahogs or surf clams, thawed

Drops of Worcestershire sauce

In a heavy 3½- to 4-quart saucepan, cook the salt pork over moderate heat until all the fat is rendered and the pork is browned, taking care not to let the pork burn. With a slotted spoon transfer the pork to drain on paper towels.

Discard all but 2 teaspoons of fat from the pan and add 1 tablespoon of the butter. Stir in the onion and sauté over moderate heat for 3 minutes, then add the celery and cook 2 or 3 minutes longer. Add the reserved salt pork, potatoes, water, clam juice, and salt and pepper to taste, and simmer, partially covered, for about 15 minutes, or until the potatoes are just tender.

While the potatoes are cooking, make a white sauce: Melt the remaining 2 tablespoons of butter in a 1-quart saucepan over moderately low heat, stir in the flour, and cook, stirring constantly, for about 3 minutes. Slowly add the milk and cook 5 minutes longer, stirring often to prevent lumps. Add this white sauce to the potatoes, add drops of Worcestershire sauce, and taste for salt and pepper.

Chill overnight, then bring back to a simmer, partially covered, for 10 minutes. Stir in the defrosted clams and just heat through. Serve hot with soda crackers.

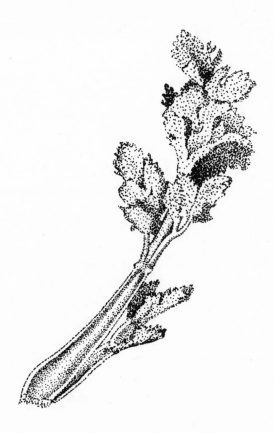

SHRIMP SOUP WITH SAFFRON AND TOMATOES

For the same deep-seated reasons that force me to freeze chicken carcasses until I have enough to make stock, I cannot throw out shrimp shells. Instead, I scrunch them down in a freezer bag, label them, and save them for this luscious cream soup. The soup can be prepared well ahead of time and finished just before serving. Rouille enriches the soup even more, but it is perfectly delicious served plain, over steamed rice or French bread toasts, or accompanied by toasted brioche.

◆

Shells from 8 ounces fresh or thawed frozen raw shrimp
1 tablespoon olive oil
2 garlic cloves, peeled and minced
3 shallots, peeled and minced
1 leek, white part only, well washed, quartered lengthwise, and thinly sliced
½ cup dry white wine
12 ounces ripe tomatoes, stemmed and roughly chopped, or 1½ cups canned crushed plum tomatoes, drained
1 teaspoon saffron threads
2 sprigs flat-leaf parsley
2 sprigs fresh thyme
1 quart Chicken Stock (page 12), or one 10½-ounce can condensed chicken broth plus enough water to equal 1 quart
1 strip orange zest
Salt
Freshly ground black pepper
Cayenne pepper (optional)
1 cup half-and-half, scalded
Rouille (page 121; optional)

Place the shrimp shells in a heavy 3-quart saucepan with the oil, garlic, and shallots. Cook over moderate heat, stirring often, until the shallots and leek are translucent and the shells are bright pink. Add the white wine and cook over high heat until it has evaporated. Add the tomatoes, saffron, parsley, thyme, chicken stock, orange zest, and salt, pepper, and cayenne (if using) to taste and bring to a boil. Lower the heat and simmer, covered, for 20 minutes.

Put the tomato base through a ricer or food mill fitted with the medium blade, pressing hard on the solids to extract all juices. The soup can be prepared ahead to this point and stored in the refrigerator or freezer.

To finish the soup, reheat the tomato base in a heavy saucepan, add the scalded half-and-half, and simmer very slowly for about 10 minutes. Taste for seasoning and serve hot, with rouille if desired.

SHRIMP AND SCALLOP CHOWDER

Prepare the tomato base as directed, or use the Tomato Fish Stock on page 16. Reheat the base to a simmer, add 8 ounces of fresh or thawed frozen medium shrimp, shelled and cut in half, and 8 ounces of sea scallops, cut into small cubes. Simmer for 2 or 3 minutes, until the fish is barely cooked, add the hot scalded half-and-half, and simmer 3 to 5 minutes longer. Serve over steamed rice. Rouille is an excellent and delicious accompaniment for this luxurious main course soup.

BEEF AND CABBAGE SOUP

Leftover beef from a stew, pot roast, or the still flavorful beef or oxtail left from making stock is the basis for this gutsy peasant soup, which tastes best when made a day in advance. Serve with dark bread and red wine or beer.

♦

2 tablespoons olive oil

1 large onion, peeled and chopped

2 medium leeks, white and 1 inch of green, trimmed, cut into ¼-inch slices, and rinsed well under lukewarm running water

3 carrots, peeled and cut into ¼-inch dice

1 large parsnip, peeled and cut into ¼-inch dice

2 to 3 cups diced cooked beef or oxtail

½ cup small dried navy beans, cooked (page 51), or 1½ cups cooked canned navy beans or cannellini beans

6 cups Brown Beef Stock (page 8), Brown Beef and Oxtail Stock (page 9), or one and a half 10½-ounce cans condensed beef broth plus enough water to equal 6 cups

2 bay leaves

1 pound green cabbage trimmed of wilted leaves, cored and shredded

2 ounces sun-dried tomatoes, cut into ¼-inch slivers

Salt

Freshly ground black pepper

Combine the oil, onion, and leeks in a large, heavy saucepan over moderate heat and sauté the vegetables for 5 minutes. Add the carrots, parsnip, beef, cooked beans, stock, and bay leaves and bring to a boil. Cover the pan, lower the heat, and simmer the soup for 30 minutes. Add the cabbage, sun-dried tomatoes, and salt and pepper to taste and continue to simmer, covered, 30 minutes longer. Remove the bay leaves before serving.

HEARTY BEEF AND VEGETABLE SOUP

This is a farmhouse soup, thick with vegetables and richly flavored with beef. **Make it a day ahead for the best flavor. Be sure to remove all the fat from the beef before cutting it into dice and adding it to the soup.**

♦

2 tablespoons vegetable oil

1 large onion, peeled and chopped

2 garlic cloves, peeled and minced

2 carrots, peeled and sliced

2 celery ribs, trimmed, halved or quartered lengthwise, and sliced

2 large potatoes, peeled and cut into ½-inch dice

2 to 3 cups diced cooked beef

6 cups Brown Beef Stock (page 8), or one 10½-ounce can condensed beef broth plus enough water to equal 6 cups

1 cup canned tomatoes with juices, coarsely chopped

Salt

Freshly ground black pepper

3 sprigs Italian parsley

1 to 2 cups fresh or frozen vegetables (lima beans, corn, green beans, peas, squash, zucchini), trimmed and cut into ½-inch pieces, if necessary

Combine the oil, onion, and garlic in a heavy 4- to 5-quart saucepan and sauté over moderate heat for 5 minutes. Add the carrots and celery and sauté 3 minutes longer. Add the potatoes, diced beef, stock, tomatoes, salt and pepper to taste, and parsley and bring the soup to a boil over high heat. Reduce the heat, partially cover the pan, and simmer the soup for 30 minutes.

Add the vegetables, taste for seasoning, and add water if the soup is becoming too thick. Simmer, partly covered, for 20 minutes longer. Remove parsley sprigs. Serve with crusty bread.

BEEF AND CABBAGE BORSCHT

One of many versions, this is hearty and ruby red, and a deeply satisfying one-dish meal. I make it a day ahead, and serve it accompanied by pumpernickel or toasted five-grain bread and cold, crisp radishes.

◆

2 tablespoons vegetable oil

1 pound lean boneless beef chuck, cut into ½-inch cubes

1 large onion, peeled, quartered, and thinly sliced

2 garlic cloves, peeled and minced

2 carrots, peeled and cut into ¼-inch dice or coarsely chopped

2 celery ribs, trimmed, quartered lengthwise, and cut into ¼-inch dice

12 ounces (about 6 medium) beets, trimmed, peeled, and cut into ¼-inch dice

12 ounces green cabbage, shredded

1 large tomato, peeled, seeded, and chopped, or 1 cup canned Italian plum tomatoes, drained and chopped

1 cup cooked white beans (drained canned cannellini are fine), or 1 medium potato, peeled and cubed

6 cups Brown Beef Stock (page 8), or one and a half 10½-ounce cans condensed beef broth plus enough water to equal 6 cups

2 or 3 sprigs fresh dill

Salt

Freshly ground black pepper

1 teaspoon sugar, or to taste

2 tablespoons wine vinegar, or to taste

Snipped fresh dill (optional)

Sour cream

Place the oil, beef chuck, onion, and garlic in a heavy 5-quart saucepan or dutch oven and place over moderately low heat. Cover the pan and cook the mixture for 20 minutes, stirring occasionally. Add the carrots, celery, beets, cabbage, tomato, white beans, stock, sprigs of dill, and salt and pepper to taste and bring the soup to a boil over moderate heat. Partially cover the pan and cook for 30 minutes, or until the meat and vegetables are tender.

Add the sugar and vinegar and simmer 10 minutes longer. Remove the dill sprigs, sprinkle each serving with snipped dill, if desired, and pass a bowl of sour cream separately.

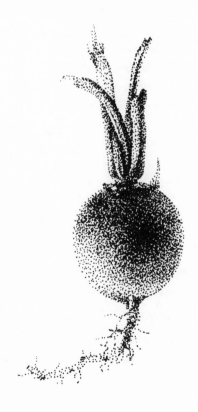

RUTH'S RATATOUILLE SOUP WITH MEATBALLS

This soup was inspired by a lovely ratatouille and spaghetti lunch my friend Ruth Gray made for me one day. Served with garlic bread and red wine it's good party fare, especially handy since it should be made a day in advance.

◆

1 eggplant (about 1 pound)
Salt
1 pound lean ground beef round
¾ cup fresh bread crumbs
2 large eggs
Freshly ground black pepper
2 teaspoons dried thyme
2 teaspoons dried oregano
3 to 4 tablespoons fruity olive oil
1 pound onions, peeled and coarsely chopped
4 large garlic cloves, peeled and minced
1 pound zucchini, trimmed and cut into ½-inch dice
1 pound mixed yellow and red bell peppers, stemmed, cored, and cut into ⅜-inch dice
One 28-ounce can imported plum tomatoes, undrained
2 quarts Roasted Vegetable Stock (page 18), Brown Beef Stock (page 8), or two 10½-ounce cans condensed beef broth plus enough water to equal 2 quarts
2 to 3 teaspoons chili powder
1 teaspoon ground cumin
2 tablespoons balsamic vinegar
4 ounces small imported Italian pasta (orecchiette, macaroni, tubetti)

Split the eggplant in half lengthwise, sprinkle the cut sides with about 1 teaspoon of salt, and let stand for 1 hour.

While the eggplant is macerating, prepare the meatballs: Place the ground beef in a mixing bowl, add the bread crumbs, eggs, 1 teaspoon of salt, a very generous grinding of black pepper, and 1 teaspoon each of the thyme and oregano, and mix with your hands until well combined. Form into small meatballs about ½ inch in diameter.

Heat 1 tablespoon of the oil in a large nonstick skillet over moderate heat, add half the meatballs and cook, shaking the pan from time to time, until they are browned on all sides. With a slotted spoon, transfer the browned meatballs to a 7- or 8-quart kettle. Brown the remaining meatballs and add them to the kettle.

Add another tablespoon of oil to the skillet, if necessary, add the onions and garlic, and sauté over moderate heat until wilted, about 5 minutes. Add the zucchini and continue cooking until the mixture is lightly browned. Transfer the mixture to the kettle.

Add 1 tablespoon of olive oil to the skillet and sauté the bell peppers until they are lightly browned, then add to the kettle. Add the tomatoes and their liquid to the skillet and cook over moderate heat for 4 or 5 minutes, crushing the tomatoes with the back of a wooden spoon and scraping up the browned bits at the bottom of the skillet. Pour the mixture into the kettle.

When the eggplant has macerated for 45 minutes, preheat the oven to 350° F.

Using paper towels, blot the moisture from the cut sides of the eggplant and place it, cut sides up, on a baking sheet. Brush the flesh with 2 teaspoons of the olive oil and bake for about 25 minutes, or until the eggplant is almost soft. Cut the flesh into ½-inch dice and add to the kettle, discarding the eggplant skin.

(continued)

Add the stock, chili powder, cumin, and salt and pepper to taste. Cover the kettle and bring the soup to a boil. Lower the heat and cook the soup, covered, for about 45 minutes. Add the vinegar and the remaining thyme and oregano, taste for salt and pepper, and continue cooking for about 15 minutes. The soup can be prepared in advance to this point.

Fifteen minutes before serving, reheat the soup. When it is boiling, add the pasta and cook for 3 or 4 minutes. Cover the kettle, remove from the stove, and let the soup stand until the pasta is cooked al dente. Serve hot with garlic bread.

PORK AND CABBAGE SOUP

MAKES ABOUT 3½ QUARTS

Pork and cabbage are a combination enshrined in peasant cooking. Here, they yield a very hearty, nourishing soup perfect for a cold night. Make this a day in advance so the flavor has time to develop.

◆

Pork Stock (page 10) made with a 3-pound loin of pork, bone in, and 4 garlic cloves; omit the bay leaf

2 tablespoons olive oil

1 large onion, peeled and finely chopped

3 garlic cloves, peeled and minced

2 carrots, peeled and diced or sliced

2 medium potatoes, peeled and diced

1½ pounds green cabbage, shredded

1½ cups imported canned plum tomatoes, drained and chopped

1 cup navy beans, soaked and cooked (page 51), or two 15-ounce cans navy beans, drained

1 bay leaf
2 or 3 sprigs Italian parsley
2 or 3 sprigs fresh thyme, or a pinch of dried thyme
2 tablespoons balsamic vinegar

Cut the pork loin in two so that it will fit neatly into the bottom of a heavy 5- to 6-quart saucepan. Make pork stock following the instructions on page 10. After the stock has cooked for 1½ hours, remove the pork from the broth, reserving the broth. Cut away the meat from the bones and return the bones to the broth. Finish cooking the stock, then cool, chill, and remove the fat as described in the recipe.

Meanwhile, cover the pork with foil and allow it to cool. Cut off and discard all the fat, cut the meat into ½-inch dice, cover well, and reserve in the refrigerator.

In a large heavy saucepan, simmer the oil, onion, and garlic, covered, over low heat for 5 minutes. Add the carrots, potatoes, cabbage, tomatoes, navy beans, diced pork, 2 quarts of pork stock, bay leaf, parsley, thyme, balsamic vinegar, and salt and pepper to taste, and bring to a boil. Reduce the heat and simmer the soup for 1 hour, partially covered. Taste for seasonings, cover, and simmer 30 minutes longer.

POZOLE

STORAGE

In the refrigerator for 2 to 3 days; frozen for up to 2 months

There are many variations of pozole, the Mexican word for both skinned white corn kernels (hominy) and for the pork or poultry soup in which the kernels are cooked. Pozole is a festive and congenial dish, particularly good for parties because each guest adds condiments and seasonings to individual taste. I can't vouch for the authenticity of this recipe, but it's delicious and easy to make. Look for dried pozole in supermarkets or health food stores. Canned whole-kernel hominy can be purchased in some supermarkets and in Mexican-American grocery stores.

◆

Pork Stock (page 10) made with a 2½- to 3-pound loin of pork, bone in, and 3 garlic cloves, plus 1 large onion, peeled and halved

1 cup dried pozole, soaked and cooked (see Note), or 3 cups drained canned whole-kernel hominy

ACCOMPANIMENTS

Chopped Bermuda or red onion
Avocado, peeled, pitted, and cut into ½-inch cubes
Juice of 1 lime
Lime wedges
Tortilla chips
Dried oregano or sprigs of fresh oregano
Chopped fresh jalapeño peppers, or dried red pepper flakes
Chopped fresh coriander

Make the pork stock following the instructions on page 10. After the stock has cooked for 1½ hours, remove the pork from the broth, reserving the broth. Cut away the meat from the bones and return the bones to the broth. Finish cooking the stock, then cool, chill, and remove the fat as described in the recipe.

Meanwhile, cover the pork with foil and allow it to cool. Cut off and discard all the fat, shred the meat or cut it into ½-inch dice, cover well, and store in the refrigerator.

Thirty minutes before serving, reheat the stock, add the hominy and pork and taste for seasoning.

Place accompaniments in separate bowls or small dishes (the herbs and hot peppers can share one little plate) and arrange on the table. To serve, ladle the hot broth with some hominy and pork into each soup bowl and have your guests add any or all of the accompaniments to their portions.

Note: Soak the dried pozole (hominy) in water to cover overnight. The next day, drain it, add 3 cups salted water, and simmer for 2½ to 3 hours.

MATZOH BALL SOUP

This is the purest kind of chicken soup—good homemade chicken stock reduced until it is very rich, with a few sliced carrots added for color, texture, and flavor 15 minutes before the soup is done. The matzoh balls are cooked separately in boiling salted water hours ahead of serving time and then reheated in the soup. The recipe makes a lot of soup, so it's perfect for festive occasions when you're entertaining family and friends.

◆

MATZOH BALLS

8 large eggs, separated

2 tablespoons chicken stock

2 tablespoons vegetable oil, preferably safflower

2 to 3 teaspoons kosher salt

Generous grating of nutmeg

3 tablespoons snipped fresh dill

2 cups matzoh meal

5 to 6 quarts Chicken Stock (page 12), with no salt added
   during cooking

2 or 3 carrots, peeled and thinly sliced

Salt

Freshly ground white pepper

TO MAKE THE MATZOH BALLS

In a large bowl, beat the egg whites with an electric mixer until moderately stiff peaks form. In another bowl, beat the egg yolks briefly with a whisk. Whisk into the yolks the stock, oil, salt, nutmeg, and dill. Fold the egg yolk mixture into the whites; the mixture will be quite soupy. Add the matzoh meal and fold in. Cover the bowl with plastic wrap and refrigerate for several hours.

Bring 5 to 6 quarts of water to a boil in a deep, wide pot. Wet your hands with lukewarm water and form the matzoh mixture into nuggets about the size of a walnut and drop them into the boiling liquid. Cover the pot, lower the heat, and simmer the matzoh balls for about 35 minutes. If made in advance, the matzoh balls can be transferred to a plate and covered with foil or plastic wrap to prevent their surface from drying out. Store in the refrigerator if you have made them a day in advance.

TO PREPARE THE CHICKEN SOUP

In a stock pot, bring the chicken stock to a boil over high heat and cook until it is reduced by one-quarter to one-third; the soup should be very flavorful. Reduce the heat, add the carrots and salt and white pepper to taste, and simmer the stock for 15 to 20 minutes. Add the matzoh balls, cook slowly until they are heated, and serve at once.

CHICKEN NOODLE SOUP WITH VEGETABLES

Packed with vegetables that have been cooked until they are tender but still tasty and full of texture, this soup makes a wonderful family dinner. Serve with heated crusty bread and follow with a fruit dessert.

◆

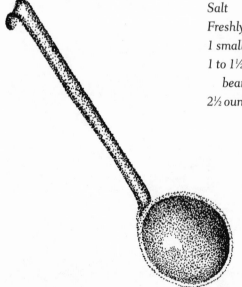

2 tablespoons unsalted butter

1 large onion, peeled and chopped

1 small leek, trimmed, halved, sliced, and rinsed (optional)

1 garlic clove, peeled and minced

1 red or green bell pepper, stemmed, seeded, and cut into ¼-inch dice

2 carrots, peeled and sliced

2 celery ribs, trimmed, halved lengthwise, and sliced

14 to 16 ounces skinless, boneless raw chicken (preferably thighs), cut into ½-inch dice, or 2 to 3 cups diced cooked chicken

6 cups Chicken Stock (page 12), or one and a half 10½-ounce cans condensed chicken broth plus enough water to equal 6 cups

Salt

Freshly ground black pepper

1 small zucchini, trimmed and diced

1 to 1½ cups frozen vegetables: green beans, corn, baby lima beans

2½ ounces dried egg noodles

Combine the butter, onion, leek (if using), and garlic in a heavy 4-quart saucepan and sauté over moderate heat for 5 minutes. Add the bell pepper and cook for 3 minutes. Stir in the carrots and celery and sauté 3 minutes longer.

If you are using raw chicken, stir it in now and sauté for 3 minutes. Add the stock and salt and pepper to taste, bring to a simmer, and cook, uncovered, for 10 minutes, or until the chicken is just cooked. Add the zucchini, frozen vegetables, and the cooked chicken, if using, and simmer, covered, for 20 minutes. Taste for seasoning.

Stir in the egg noodles, cover the pan, and turn off the heat. Let the soup stand for 10 minutes, or until the noodles are tender.

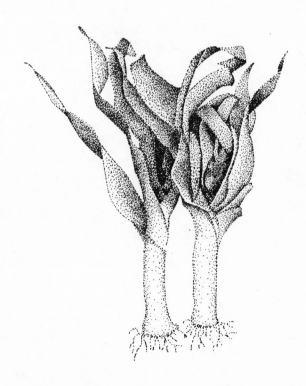

CURRIED CREAM OF CHICKEN SOUP WITH APPLES AND ONIONS

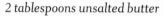

Pale yellow with tiny flecks of red pepper and the subtle flavor of apple, this soup can be made very quickly. If you are cooking chicken especially for the soup, boneless, skinless thighs are a good choice because they don't dry out as readily as the breast does. Leftover turkey and turkey stock are delicious substitutes for chicken.

♦

2 tablespoons unsalted butter

2 large garlic cloves, peeled and minced

1 large sweet onion, peeled and chopped

1 small jalapeño pepper, stemmed, partially seeded, and minced (optional)

1 small green or red bell pepper, stemmed, seeded, and chopped

2 large Granny Smith or other tart apples, peeled, cored, and coarsely chopped

1½ to 2 teaspoons curry powder

1½ tablespoons flour

2 teaspoons minced fresh ginger

1 quart Chicken Stock (page 12), Turkey Stock (page 11), or one 10½-ounce can condensed chicken broth plus enough water to equal 1 quart

Salt

Freshly ground pepper

2 cups diced cooked chicken or turkey

1 cup half-and-half

Combine the butter, garlic, and onion in a heavy 3-quart saucepan and sauté over moderate heat for 5 minutes. Add the jalapeño, if desired, and the bell pepper and sauté for 5 minutes. Add the apples and curry powder and cook for 3 minutes, stirring often.

Sprinkle the mixture with the flour and sauté for 2 to 3 minutes, or until the flour is cooked. Stir in the ginger, chicken stock, add salt and pepper to taste, and bring to a boil over high heat. Reduce the heat and simmer the soup for 15 minutes, partially covered. Add the chicken and simmer 5 minutes longer. Stir in the half-and-half and cook for 5 minutes. Taste for seasoning again, and serve at once.

TURKEY AND BARLEY SOUP

. . . .

MAKES 9 TO 10 CUPS

This is a natural to make after Thanksgiving or Christmas, when the turkey carcass and a lot of usable scraps are staring at you reproachfully. The richly flavored stock and piquant seasonings overcome the blandness of the barley. When reheating frozen soup, taste for spiciness, because the strength of the cumin and cayenne tends to fade with freezing.

◆

2 tablespoons butter or vegetable oil

1 large 7- to 8-ounce onion, chopped

3 celery stalks, thinly sliced

2 carrots, peeled, quartered, and thinly sliced

2 cups diced cooked turkey

4 ounces canned sliced pimientos

½ cup uncooked barley

2 quarts Turkey Stock (page 11), Chicken Stock (page 12), or two 10½-ounce cans condensed chicken broth and enough water to equal 2 quarts

½ teaspoon Cajun seasoning, or ⅛ teaspoon cayenne pepper plus ⅛ teaspoon ground cumin

½ teaspoon dried oregano or basil

Salt

Freshly ground white or black pepper

In a heavy 4- to 5-quart saucepan, melt the butter or heat the oil over moderate heat. Add the onion and sauté until translucent. Add the celery and carrots and sauté for 2 minutes. Add the turkey, pimiento, barley, and stock and bring to a boil over high heat. Stir in the cayenne, cumin, oregano, and salt and pepper to taste and cover the pan. Reduce the heat to low and simmer the soup for about 1 hour, or until the barley is very tender. Adjust the seasonings and serve hot.

TURKEY, WILD RICE, AND VEGETABLE SOUP

. . . .

MAKES A GENEROUS 2 QUARTS

The crunchy texture of wild rice
contrasts nicely with the tender
vegetables, but because the rice
becomes soggy as it absorbs the hot
liquid, the soup is best eaten at
once. Since the rice is cooked
separately and added just before
serving, however, the soup itself
can be made well in advance.

◆

1½ tablespoons unsalted butter
1 medium onion, peeled and chopped
2 stalks celery, quartered lengthwise and sliced
2 carrots, peeled and diced
2 cups diced cooked turkey or chicken
2 cups diced winter squash (Hubbard, acorn, or other)
2 quarts Turkey Stock (page 11), Chicken Stock (page 12), or
     two 10½-ounce cans condensed chicken broth plus enough
     water to equal 2 quarts
1 bay leaf
Salt
Freshly ground white or black pepper
2 or 3 fresh sage leaves, or ½ teaspoon dried sage, crumbled
1 cup frozen tiny peas
½ cup raw wild rice, cooked until just tender

Melt the butter in a 4-quart heavy-bottomed saucepan over
moderate heat. Add the onion and sauté until translucent.
Add the celery, carrots, turkey, squash, stock, bay leaf, salt
and pepper to taste, and sage and bring to a boil over high
heat. Partially cover the pan, reduce the heat, and simmer
the soup for 30 minutes.

Five minutes before the soup is done, add the peas and
cooked wild rice and taste for seasoning. If you've used fresh
sage leaves, remove them and the bay leaf. Serve hot.

BEAN SOUPS

· ·

Hearty, flavorful, nutritious, and inexpensive, bean soups are a happy and healthy choice for family meals. Blissfully easy to prepare, most bean soups taste even better made in advance, and they freeze well. I buy my beans in health food stores, supermarkets, and in gourmet food stores and Italian food markets, the latter two being good sources for specialty beans—cannellini, sweet runners, green French lentils, and others.

All these soups can be stored in the refrigerator for 2 or 3 days, or frozen for up to 2 months. It is especially important to check (and, if necessary, revitalize) the flavor of previously frozen bean soups, or they will be too bland.

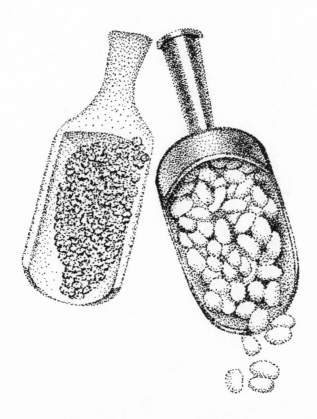

COOKING DRIED BEANS

SOAKING

Lentils and dried split peas are the only exceptions to the rule that all dried beans need soaking. Measure the beans, then pick them over and discard imperfect beans and any small stones. Place the beans in a strainer and rinse them well under cold running water, then drain them.

Quick soaking: Place the beans in a saucepan with cold water to cover by 2 inches. Bring the beans to a boil over high heat, boil for 1 minute, and remove from the heat. Cover the pan and allow the beans to soak for 1 hour.

Overnight soaking: Place the beans in a saucepan or bowl, pour in cold water to cover by 2 inches, and allow the beans to soak for about 8 hours.

COOKING

Drain the beans in a strainer, rinse under cold running water, and place in a saucepan with enough fresh cold water to cover by 2 inches. During the initial cooking (until the beans are tender), neither salt nor acid ingredients such as tomatoes, lemon juice, and vinegar, should be added to the cooking liquid. Seasoning and flavorings are added later. (To make Bean Stock, follow the instructions on page 19.) Bring the water to a slow boil, lower the heat, and simmer slowly, covered, until the beans are tender. Add salt to taste and cook 5 minutes longer. Drain the beans and use as directed in the recipe.

Spicy Bean Soup with Rice and Greens

Make the soup a day in advance, then simply reheat it while you cook the rice and greens. For a milder flavor, use a little less cayenne.

◆

½ cup dried red kidney beans, soaked, drained, and rinsed (page 51)

½ cup dried cannellini beans, soaked, drained, and rinsed (page 51)

2½ quarts water

An 8-ounce ham bone or smoked ham hock

½ teaspoon cayenne pepper

½ teaspoon ground cumin

½ teaspoon freshly ground black pepper

½ teaspoon ground dried thyme

2 bay leaves

2 tablespoons unsalted butter or vegetable oil

1 large onion, peeled and chopped

2 garlic cloves, peeled and minced

1 large green bell pepper, stemmed, seeded, and chopped

¾ cup chopped celery

Salt

Hot cooked white rice

Steamed or sautéed greens (mustard, turnip, kale, or arugula)

Place the kidney and cannellini beans in a 5-quart saucepan, add the water, ham bone, cayenne, cumin, black pepper, thyme, and bay leaves, and bring to a boil over high heat. Cover the pan and simmer over low heat for about 1 hour, or until the beans are very tender. Remove the ham bone from the soup and strip off and shred all the meat. Discard the bone and gristle and return the meat to the soup.

Meanwhile, melt the butter in a heavy skillet, add the onion and garlic, and cook over moderate heat until golden brown, 6 or 7 minutes. Add the green pepper and sauté 3 to 4 minutes longer. Add the onion and pepper mixture, the celery, and salt to the soup and continue cooking, covered, for 25 minutes.

The soup will be quite thin. To serve, spoon hot rice and cooked greens into soup plates and ladle in the soup.

JUDY'S BEAN MIX

MAKES 1 POUND MIXED BEANS

STORAGE
In tightly sealed plastic bags,
tins, or jars

There are many different prepackaged bean mixes, most of them excellent, sold nationwide in supermarkets, specialty food stores, and health food stores. It betrays a certain compulsiveness on my part that I actually went out and shopped for thirteen or fourteen kinds of dried beans and legumes, then sat down one afternoon and measured them out in what turned out to be an attractive and tasty mixture, which I then replicated a number of times for gifts. The mix is worth making only in quantity, so if you have a scale that measures in fractions of ounces and a child who's willing to spend an afternoon measuring and packing thousands of beans in plastic bags, tins, and jars for you and other loved ones, try this combination:

2 ounces black beans
1.75 ounces pink and kidney beans
1.5 ounces yellow split peas
1.5 ounces green split peas
1.5 ounces barley
1.25 ounces small navy beans
1.25 ounces small black-eyed peas
1.25 ounces lentils
1 ounce pintos
.75 ounce mung
.75 ounce baby limas
.75 ounce garbanzos
.75 ounce adzukis

JUDY'S BEAN SOUP

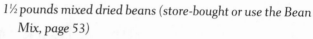

MAKES 7 1/2 TO 8 QUARTS

This is my standby soup, the one people crave, the one I keep on hand to heat up for unexpected guests. It is also the perfect main course for a buffet dinner party. Make it a day ahead. Serve it with crusty bread, salad, and red wine or beer.

◆

1½ pounds mixed dried beans (store-bought or use the Bean Mix, page 53)

1 to 1¼ pounds smoked ham hocks or 12 to 16 ounces cured ham

6 quarts water

¼ cup balsamic vinegar

3 or 4 bay leaves

1 teaspoon black peppercorns

4 or 5 whole cloves

5 tablespoons olive oil

8 to 10 garlic cloves, peeled and finely chopped (optional)

6 medium onions, peeled and chopped

One 28-ounce can imported peeled plum tomatoes, with juices, coarsely chopped

1 pound carrots, peeled, quartered lengthwise, and sliced

1 small bunch celery, with tops, root ends trimmed, each rib quartered lengthwise and sliced

1 large sprig fresh rosemary

Salt

Freshly ground black pepper

1¼ pounds raw boneless turkey or chicken, cut into ½-inch dice

5 medium new potatoes, scrubbed and cut into ⅜-inch dice

Freshly grated Parmesan cheese (optional)

Place the beans (no need to soak them), ham hocks, water, 2 tablespoons of the vinegar, bay leaves, peppercorns, and cloves in a 12-quart stock pot, cover, and bring to a boil over high heat. Reduce the heat and simmer, covered, for 2½ hours.

Meanwhile, in a large skillet, heat the olive oil over moderate heat, add the garlic and onions, and sauté for about 8 minutes, or until the onions begin to turn golden. When the beans have cooked for 2½ hours, add the garlic and onions, tomatoes, carrots, celery, rosemary, and salt and pepper to taste, and simmer for 1 hour.

Remove the ham hocks and strip off all the usable scraps of meat, discarding the bones and gristle. Shred the meat fine and return it to the soup. Add the turkey and potatoes and cook 30 to 60 minutes longer. Remove the rosemary sprig, add the remaining balsamic vinegar, and taste for salt and pepper. Serve with Parmesan cheese, if desired.

OPTIONAL GARNISH
FOR 6 TO 8 PEOPLE

1 large bunch kale or mustard greens
2 tablespoons fruity olive oil
¼ to ½ teaspoon dried red pepper flakes (optional)
2 or 3 large garlic cloves, peeled and coarsely chopped
Freshly grated Parmesan cheese

Cut off and wash the kale leaves and cut them crosswise into 1-inch strips. Place the leaves in a colander, rinse, and drain.

Heat the olive oil in a large skillet or saucepan over moderate heat, add the red pepper flakes, if using, and the garlic and stir for about 1 minute. Add the kale and stir to coat with the oil and garlic mixture, then cover and cook until the vegetable is wilted but not totally limp.

Stir the vegetable mixture into 3½ to 4 quarts of hot soup and cook for about 20 minutes, or until the flavors have blended. Taste for seasoning. Serve in soup bowls and pass a bowl of grated Parmesan cheese.

BLACK BEAN AND PEPPERONI SOUP

A Super Bowl Sunday kind of soup, good with beer, corn chips, tostadas, or corn bread. It should be made a day in advance. I generally chop the vegetables for the soffrito in the food processor. The combination of red, yellow, and green bell peppers floating in the black beans looks enticing and tastes even better.

◆

2½ cups dried black beans, soaked, rinsed, and drained (page 51)

3½ quarts water

4½ cups Brown Beef Stock (page 8) or one 10½-ounce can of concentrated beef broth plus enough water to equal 4½ cups

Salt

Freshly ground pepper

½ cup fruity olive oil

2 large sweet onions, peeled and chopped

5 or more garlic cloves, peeled and finely chopped

2 large red bell peppers, cored, seeded, and chopped

2 large green bell peppers, cored, seeded, and chopped

2 large yellow bell peppers, cored, seeded, and chopped

6 to 8 celery stalks, chopped or sliced

4 medium tomatoes, peeled and chopped

1 pound pepperoni, casings removed, very thinly sliced

1 teaspoon hot pepper flakes

2 tablespoons red wine vinegar

GARNISH

3 cups sour cream

1 bunch scallions, trimmed and finely sliced

1 bunch cilantro, stems discarded and leaves finely chopped

Place the beans in a 12-quart stock pot with the water and bring to a boil over high heat. Lower the heat and simmer, partially covered, for 1½ to 2 hours, or until they are tender. Add the beef stock 30 minutes before the beans are cooked. Add salt and pepper to taste, then cook 5 minutes longer.

Meanwhile, make the soffrito: In a large, heavy saucepan, combine the olive oil, onions, and garlic and sauté over moderate heat until translucent, about 8 minutes. Add the bell peppers and celery and cook until slightly softened, about 4 minutes longer. Add the tomatoes and cook just until they have released their juices, 3 to 4 minutes. Set aside.

When the beans are tender, stir in the soffrito, pepperoni, hot pepper flakes, salt and pepper to taste, and vinegar, return the soup to a simmer, and cook 30 minutes longer.

In a mixing bowl, combine the sour cream, scallions, and cilantro and transfer to a serving bowl. Serve the sour cream with the soup and hot corn bread.

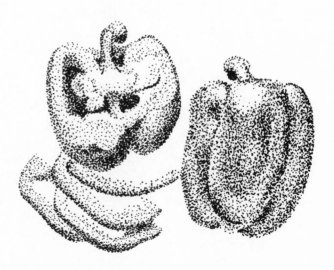

CANNELLINI BEAN AND GARLIC SOUP

MAKES 2½ TO 3 QUARTS

Cannellini beans are white, similar in appearance to navy beans, but somewhat larger and considerably more flavorful. The beans are imported from Italy and available at Italian groceries, specialty food stores, and by mail order. This soup is thick and hearty, sweetened by the many garlic cloves that cook with the beans. Make it a day ahead so the flavor develops, and serve with a crusty Italian or French bread; follow with a salad, cheese, and fruit.

◆

1 head garlic (at least 10 cloves)
1 pound cannellini beans, soaked, drained, and rinsed
   (page 51)
3 quarts water
2 bay leaves
3 sprigs Italian parsley
2 sprigs fresh thyme or rosemary, or a large pinch of dried
   thyme or rosemary
2 tablespoons fruity olive oil
2 medium onions, peeled and chopped
3 carrots, peeled and cut into small dice
10 ounces green beans, trimmed and cut into ½-inch lengths
1 ounce sun-dried tomatoes, cut into fine slivers
Salt
Freshly ground white or black pepper
1½ tablespoons balsamic or red wine vinegar

OPTIONAL GARNISHES

Green Sauce (page 119), or extra-virgin olive oil and freshly
   grated Parmesan cheese, or sautéed finely chopped
   prosciutto or pancetta

Separate the garlic cloves, crush them with the flat of a large knife, and discard the skins. Place the garlic, beans, water, bay leaves, parsley, and thyme in a heavy 5- to 6-quart saucepan and bring the mixture to a boil over high heat. Reduce the heat and simmer the beans gently, partially covered, for 1 hour.

Heat the olive oil in a skillet over moderate heat, add the onions, and sauté for 5 minutes. Add the onions, carrots, green beans, and sun-dried tomatoes to the beans. Season very moderately with salt and pepper to taste and simmer, covered, for 40 to 60 minutes. Taste for seasoning again and add the vinegar to bring up the flavors. Cook a few minutes longer and serve with one of the garnishes, if you wish.

V A R I A T I O N S

• Other beans to use: lentils, with or without chopped parsnip; chick-peas; black beans or kidney beans with tiny pieces of chorizo, Chinese sausage, or pepperoni, chopped coriander, and some lime juice.

• Other vegetables to add: shredded cabbage, added with onions and carrots; sautéed escarole or chard added during last 15 minutes of cooking; chopped spinach added during last 5 minutes; fresh or frozen green peas, especially good with black beans and Chinese sausage and garlic.

• Add smoked pork, ham, or bacon—delicious with shredded cabbage.

CHICK-PEA AND SAUSAGE SOUP WITH GREENS

MAKES 3 ½ TO 4 QUARTS

I like a little spice in my life and that's why I use all hot sausages in this soup, but a combination of sweet and hot or all sweet sausages is just as wonderful. Make the soup a day ahead, and serve with a crusty Italian bread.

◆

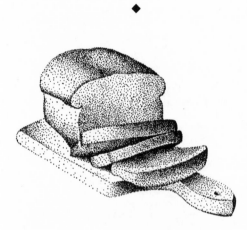

2 tablespoons olive oil
1 pound hot Italian sausages, removed from their casings
2 medium onions, peeled and chopped
3 to 5 cloves garlic, crushed with the flat of a knife and peeled
3 carrots, peeled and sliced
2 celery ribs, trimmed, quartered lengthwise, and sliced
2 cups dried chick-peas, soaked and cooked with 1 bay leaf
    (page 51), 2 cups cooking liquid reserved
1 quart Chicken Stock (page 12), or one 10½-ounce can
    condensed chicken broth plus enough water to equal 1 quart
One 28-ounce can imported Italian plum tomatoes, crushed
    with their juices
3 or 4 sprigs Italian parsley
2 sprigs fresh oregano
1 teaspoon fennel seeds (optional)
Salt
Freshly ground black pepper
2 quarts shredded kale leaves, rinsed and drained

Heat the olive oil in a heavy 6-quart saucepan over moderate heat, add the sausage and brown it, stirring to break up the meat with a wooden spoon. Add the onions and garlic and sauté until they are translucent, 3 or 4 minutes, scraping up the caramelized sausage from the bottom of the pan. Add carrots and celery and sauté 3 or 4 minutes longer. Add the cooked chick-peas with their reserved cooking liquid, chicken broth, tomatoes, parsley, oregano, fennel seeds if using, and salt and pepper to taste and bring the soup to a boil over high heat. Reduce the heat, partially cover the pan, and simmer the soup slowly for 1½ hours.

Add the kale to the soup and continue cooking for 30 minutes. Remove the herb sprigs and serve the soup hot.

LEMON LENTIL SOUP

This elegant soup is dedicated to Pam Marron, who ate most of the first batch I made right out of the saucepan. The soup tastes just fine made with canned condensed chicken broth diluted with water, but for special occasions it deserves your best homemade chicken stock and green French lentils. It's really good served chilled.

◆

1 tablespoon unsalted butter
1 small onion, peeled and chopped
1 or 2 carrots, peeled and coarsely chopped
1 celery rib, trimmed and coarsely chopped
½ cup green French lentils or brown lentils, picked over and rinsed
1 quart Chicken Stock (page 12), or one 10½-ounce can of condensed chicken broth plus enough water to equal 1 quart
Two 3-inch strips lemon zest
3 or 4 sprigs fresh thyme (preferably lemon thyme)
1 sprig Italian parsley
1 bay leaf
Salt
Freshly ground black pepper
Drops of fresh lemon juice
Sour Cream Sauce (page 122)

Melt the butter in a heavy-bottomed 2-quart saucepan over moderate heat, add the onions, and sauté for 2 minutes. Add the carrots and celery and continue to cook until the onion is translucent, another 3 minutes or so. Add the lentils, stock, lemon zest, thyme, parsley, and bay leaf and bring to a low boil over moderately high heat. Cover the saucepan, lower the heat, and simmer the soup gently for about 50 minutes, adding salt and pepper to taste during the last 15 minutes of cooking.

Remove the bay leaf, transfer the soup in batches to a blender, and purée. (The French lentils will not disintegrate completely, but the brown lentils will.) Add drops of lemon juice to taste. Serve the soup hot, warm, or chilled. Swirl sour cream sauce into each serving.

LENTIL, YAM, AND TOMATO SOUP WITH GREENS

MAKES A GENEROUS 4 QUARTS

MAKES A GENEROUS 4 QUARTS

You could write a book about lentil soup. Here's one from the recipe archives of Ethel Hultberg.

The lentil, yam, and tomato base is colorful and delicious on its own, but the soup looks more festive, tastes even better, and is healthier with at least some of the greens added. Use moderate amounts and don't overload the soup. Add water or stock to thin out the mixture, if necessary. This recipe makes 4 quarts of base, which freezes well. You can also halve the recipe easily. And be sure to make the soup a day ahead for the best flavor.

◆

BASE

2 cups brown or green lentils

2 medium onions, peeled and chopped

4 garlic cloves, peeled and chopped

2 or 3 celery ribs, trimmed, quartered lengthwise, and sliced

3 carrots, peeled, halved lengthwise, and sliced

2 medium yams or sweet potatoes, peeled and cut into ½-inch dice

One 28-ounce can imported Italian plum tomatoes, with juices, the tomatoes coarsely chopped

2 quarts Roasted Vegetable Stock (page 18), Chicken Stock (page 12), or two 10½-ounce cans condensed chicken broth plus enough water to equal 2 quarts

3 bay leaves

2 sprigs of fresh thyme, or 1 sprig fresh rosemary (optional)

Salt

Freshly ground black pepper to taste

ADDITIONS

Stock or water

Pickled peperoncini, stemmed, seeded, and coarsely chopped

Frozen tiny peas

Arugula, watercress, spinach, or escarole leaves, well washed and finely shredded

Scallions, root ends and green tips trimmed, thinly sliced

A handful of Italian parsley leaves, washed, patted dry, and chopped

OPTIONAL GARNISH

Fruity olive oil

Freshly grated Parmesan cheese

To make the base, place the lentils, onions, garlic, celery, carrots, sweet potatoes, tomatoes, stock, and bay leaves in a large soup kettle and bring to a boil over high heat, crushing the tomatoes with the back of a spoon. Cover the kettle, lower the heat, and simmer the soup for about 1 hour, or until the lentils are very tender, checking from time to time to see that there is enough liquid and adding water as required. Add herb sprigs, if you like, and salt and pepper to taste after the soup has cooked for 30 minutes. The soup base can be made ahead to this point. To store, remove the bay leaves and thyme or rosemary, allow the soup to cool to room temperature uncovered, then refrigerate or freeze it, tightly covered.

ADDITIONS

The soup will thicken as it stands. Reheat it slowly, stirring from the bottom often to keep the soup base from sticking to the kettle, and adding stock or water, if necessary. When the soup is at a slow boil, stir in the peperoncini and cook for about 5 minutes. Add the peas, arugula, scallions, and parsley and return to a boil. Taste the soup for seasoning, remove the bay leaves if you haven't done so, and serve drizzled with olive oil and sprinkled with grated Parmesan, if you wish. Delicious hot or warm, and even tastier the next day.

VARIATIONS

This soup lends itself to infinite variations and additions.

FLAVORINGS

• Add cumin and cayenne pepper to taste at the beginning of cooking. Substitute chopped fresh coriander for the parsley or use it in addition to parsley.

(continued)

Lentil, Yam, and Tomato Soup with Greens *(continued)*

• Add curry powder at the beginning of cooking. Serve the soup with a dollop of plain yogurt.

MEATS

• Add 8 ounces thinly sliced veal sausages to the soup at the beginning of cooking.
• Add 4 to 8 ounces thinly sliced pepperoni or chorizo toward end of cooking.
• Add a ham bone or smoked ham hock at the start of cooking. Remove the bone at the end of cooking, strip off and shred the meat, and add it to the soup.

VEGETABLE ADDITIONS

• Use 1 cup lentils and 1 cup of a dried bean of your choice that has been soaked and cooked (page 51).
• Finely shredded cabbage, kale, or Swiss chard leaves can be added 15 minutes before the end of cooking.
• Add sliced zucchini or summer squash toward the end of cooking. Use shredded fresh basil leaves with or instead of the parsley.
• After 30 minutes of cooking time, stir in green beans, trimmed, and cut into ½-inch lengths.
• Use well-washed and shredded white of leeks in addition to or instead of the onions.

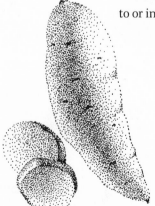

Sweet Runner Bean Soup

Sweet runners are large white beans that resemble limas but have an especially sweet flavor. Look for them in health food stores or specialty food stores. This soup tastes best if made a day in advance.

◆

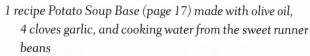

1 recipe Potato Soup Base (page 17) made with olive oil, 4 cloves garlic, and cooking water from the sweet runner beans
5 ounces dried sweet runner beans, cooked (page 51) and drained, 1 quart cooking liquid reserved
2 medium carrots, peeled and cut into ¼-inch dice
3 or 4 sun-dried tomatoes, cut into thin slivers
Salt
Freshly ground black pepper
1 or 2 sprigs fresh rosemary
Fruity olive oil
Freshly grated Parmesan cheese

Combine the potato soup base, cooked beans, carrots, sun-dried tomatoes, salt and pepper to taste, and the rosemary in a 3-quart saucepan. Bring the soup to a simmer, cover, and cook at a very slow simmer for 45 to 60 minutes. Remove rosemary sprigs and serve warm drizzled with olive oil and sprinkled with Parmesan cheese.

PASTA E FAGIOLI

One of the classic Italian soups, this, like so many others, tastes even better the next day. I've made it with freshly cooked dried beans, imported canned beans, and beans canned in the United States, and truth to tell, the first two are the best. I've also made it with all kidney beans and all cannellinis and added shredded greens, such as kale or mustard or turnip greens, toward the end of cooking.

◆

1 tablespoon olive oil, plus some for garnish

4 ounces pancetta or lean salt pork, cut into ¼-inch dice

1 large onion, peeled and chopped

3 or 4 garlic cloves, peeled and minced

1 celery rib, trimmed and chopped

1 carrot, peeled and chopped

½ cup each dried cannellini beans, kidney beans, and chick-peas, cooked (page 51), ¾ cup cooking liquid reserved

Half a 28-ounce can imported Italian plum tomatoes, with juices, coarsely chopped

2 cups Brown Beef Stock (page 8), Chicken Stock (page 12), or half a 10½-ounce can condensed beef or chicken broth plus enough water to equal 2 cups

1 sprig Italian parsley

1 small sprig fresh rosemary

1 bay leaf

Salt

Freshly ground black pepper

Generous ½ cup small pasta (preferably imported), such as tubetti, shells, or elbow macaroni

Freshly grated Parmesan cheese

Combine 1 tablespoon of the oil and the pancetta in a heavy 3½- to 4-quart saucepan and sauté over moderate heat until the pancetta has rendered its fat and is browned; do not allow it to burn. (If using salt pork instead of pancetta, pour out all but 1 tablespoon of the fat.) Add the onion and garlic and sauté for 3 minutes. Add the celery and carrot and sauté 3 minutes longer.

Meanwhile, in a food processor fitted with the steel blade, purée 1½ cups of the cooked beans with ¾ cup of cooking liquid. Add the bean purée, the remaining beans, tomatoes, stock, parsley, rosemary, bay leaf, and salt and pepper to taste to the sautéed vegetables and pancetta. Stir well and bring to a simmer. Cover the saucepan and simmer the soup over low heat for 25 minutes. Add the pasta, stir well, and cover the pan. Turn off the heat and allow the pasta to cook for about 10 minutes. Remove the herb sprigs and bay leaf and serve the soup hot or at room temperature with a basket of crusty peasant bread. Pass olive oil and Parmesan separately.

PASTA E FAGIOLI WITH CANNED BEANS

Use three 20-ounce cans of imported dried beans or three 15- or 16-ounce cans of beans produced in the United States. Drain the beans, reserving about 6 ounces of the canning liquid. Rinse the beans briefly under running water, drain, and place 1½ cups of beans, the reserved 6 ounces of liquid and 6 ounces of water in the food processor. Purée the mixture and continue with the recipe. If you are using imported canned beans, add an additional ½ to 1 cup of stock to the soup to accommodate the larger amount of beans.

CLASSIC SPLIT PEA SOUP

The texture of this homey soup can be varied by reserving ½ cup of the split peas and adding them during the last 45 minutes of cooking. Halve the recipe if you need only 5 or 6 cups and are short of storage space.

◆

2 tablespoons vegetable oil
3 large garlic cloves, peeled and finely chopped
2 large onions, peeled and chopped
4 carrots, peeled and coarsely chopped
2 celery ribs, trimmed and coarsely chopped
2½ cups green split peas, rinsed and drained
1 pound smoked ham hocks or a meaty ham bone
2½ quarts water
1 bay leaf
Salt
Freshly ground pepper
Milk or half-and-half (optional)

Combine the oil, garlic, and onions in a heavy 5-quart soup kettle or saucepan and sauté for 5 minutes over moderate heat, or until the onions are translucent. Add the carrots and celery and stir for 1 minute, then add the split peas, ham hocks, water, bay leaf, and salt and pepper to taste. Do not salt too heavily, because the ham hocks may be very salty. Cover the pot and bring to a simmer. Simmer the soup for about 1½ hours, stirring from time to time and taking care that the bottom of the pan does not scorch. Thin with milk or half-and-half, if desired.

Remove the ham hocks, shred the meat, and discard the bones and gristle. Discard the bay leaf. If you like, you can purée all or part of the soup in batches in a food processor, or leave it as is. Return the meat to the soup and serve very hot.

CURRIED SPLIT PEA SOUP

. . . .

MAKES ABOUT 6 CUPS

This was the soup my mother always made when I visited her in Vermont, so it's very nostalgic for me. She served it with her own thickly sliced whole wheat bread, which she toasted in the oven. Barley gives the soup a nice texture. Make it a day in advance.

◆

1 tablespoon vegetable oil or butter
2 garlic cloves, peeled and finely chopped
1 medium onion, peeled and chopped
1 to 1½ teaspoons curry powder, or to taste
2 carrots, peeled and coarsely chopped
1 cup green split peas, picked over and rinsed
6 cups Roasted Vegetable Stock (page 18), Chicken Stock
    (page 12), or one and a half 10½-ounce cans condensed
    chicken broth plus enough water to equal 6 cups
1 bay leaf
Scant 2 tablespoons pearl barley, rinsed
Salt
Freshly ground black pepper

Warm the oil over moderate heat in a heavy 2½-quart saucepan, add the garlic and onions, and sauté for 5 minutes. Add the curry powder and continue to cook, stirring often, until the onions are lightly browned, about 3 minutes. Add the carrots, split peas, stock, and bay leaf and bring to a boil. Lower the heat and cook the soup, partially covered, at a slow simmer for 45 minutes.

Add the barley and salt and pepper to taste and continue cooking for 45 minutes longer, stirring from time to time to keep the soup from sticking to the bottom of the pan and adding water as needed. Taste the soup for seasoning, and remove the bay leaf before serving. If the soup cools before serving, stir well before reheating and add water or milk to thin, if necessary.

MINTED THREE-PEA SOUP

. . . .

MAKES A GENEROUS 2 QUARTS

The soup's color is bright pea green flecked with orange; its texture is creamy, punctuated by the delicious crunch of sugar snaps; and its flavor is mildly minty, but not too insistent, brought up by chopped fresh mint garnish. You can cook the soup ahead of time and freeze the base, then add the sugar snaps just before serving.

◆

1 tablespoon unsalted butter or vegetable oil

1 medium onion, peeled and chopped

2 carrots, peeled and chopped

1½ cups dried green split peas, picked over and rinsed

7 cups Roasted Vegetable Stock (page 18), Chicken Stock (page 12), or two 10½-ounce cans condensed chicken broth plus enough water to equal 7 cups

2 sprigs fresh thyme or ½ teaspoon dried thyme leaves

2 sprigs Italian parsley

Salt

Freshly ground white pepper

1 cup shelled fresh green peas or frozen tiny green peas

1 or 2 sprigs fresh mint, plus chopped mint leaves for garnish

1 cup milk or half-and-half

5 to 6 ounces sugar snap peas or 3 to 4 ounces snow peas, strings removed, thinly sliced

Plain nonfat yogurt (optional)

Melt the butter over moderately low heat in a heavy 4- to 5-quart saucepan or soup kettle. Add the onion and sauté until translucent. Add the carrots, split peas, and stock. If you are using fresh thyme sprigs, tie them to the parsley and add to the kettle with salt and pepper to taste. Bring the soup to a boil, lower the heat, and simmer slowly for 1 hour and 15 minutes, stirring from time to time and checking to see that the peas do not stick to the bottom of the pan. Add the mint sprigs and cook 5 minutes longer. Add the fresh or frozen peas and cook for 10 minutes.

Remove the thyme sprigs, parsley, and mint and purée the soup in batches in a food processor fitted with the steel blade. Return the soup to the kettle, add the milk, and bring to a slow simmer. Cook for 5 minutes, then taste for seasoning. The soup can be prepared ahead to this time and refrigerated or frozen in airtight containers.

To serve, reheat the soup slowly, stirring often from the bottom to prevent sticking. Add the sugar snap peas and simmer the soup, uncovered, for 5 minutes, or until the peas are barely cooked. (Snow peas should cook for only 2 minutes.) Serve with a spoonful of yogurt, if you wish, and sprinkle with the chopped mint leaves.

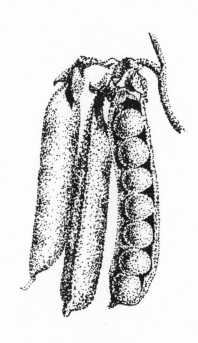

VEGETABLE SOUPS

· ·

Most of the soups in this chapter are substantial; although you can use them for starters, I've served most of them as one-course lunches or dinners. Fresh vegetables provide endless possibilities for soup, from year-round staples to seasonal arrivals. These are some of my favorites. Again, you can store most of them in the refrigerator for 2 or 3 days, or freeze them for up to 2 months, except as noted in individual recipes. Taste critically when reheating a frozen soup—you may need to do some doctoring to regain its original zip.

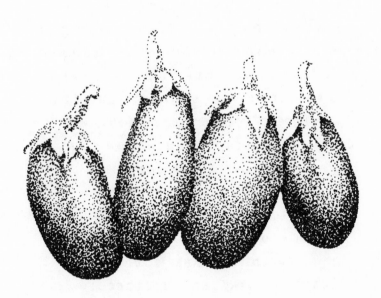

BASIC VEGETABLE SOUP

This is a casual soup, easily adapted to seasonal produce. I use the food processor to chop all the vegetables, although you might want to dice them by hand for a more professional-looking presentation. Serve with French baguettes or garlic bread.

♦

2 tablespoons olive oil

1 large garlic clove, peeled and finely chopped

1 medium onion, peeled and chopped

1 medium leek, white only, quartered lengthwise, thinly sliced, rinsed, and drained

2 medium red-skinned potatoes, unpeeled, coarsely chopped

2 medium carrots, peeled and coarsely chopped

1 medium yellow squash, ends trimmed and coarsely chopped

5 canned Italian plum tomatoes, with juices (about 1⅓ cups)

4½ cups Roasted Vegetable Stock (page 18), Chicken Stock (page 12), or one 10½-ounce can condensed chicken broth and enough water to equal 4½ cups

5 sprigs Italian parsley

Salt

Freshly ground black pepper

8 ounces fresh spinach, stem ends trimmed, well washed and drained, coarsely chopped

Freshly grated Parmesan cheese

Combine the oil, garlic, onion, and leek in a heavy 3- to 4-quart saucepan and sauté over moderate heat for 5 minutes. Add the potatoes, carrots, squash, tomatoes, stock, parsley, and salt and pepper to taste. Bring the soup to a low boil, cover, and lower the heat. Simmer the soup for 40 minutes. The soup can be made ahead to this point. Remove the parsley sprigs and store.

Just before serving, reheat the soup to a low boil, add the spinach, and simmer for 2 minutes, or just until the spinach is cooked. Serve with grated cheese on the side.

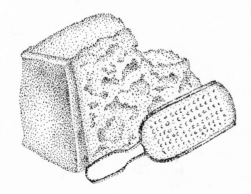

(continued)

V A R I A T I O N S

• Instead of leeks, use an additional onion and a few finely chopped shallots.

• Add 5 or 6 ounces green beans, trimmed and cut into ½-inch lengths, with the carrots and squash.

• Add 2 cups shredded green cabbage with the carrots and squash.

• Zucchini is a good substitute for or addition to summer squash, or use 8 ounces of chopped raw pumpkin.

• Add a small sweet potato, peeled and coarsely chopped.

• Five minutes before serving, add the kernels from 1 ear of corn, then add the greens 3 minutes later.

• Use fresh, flavorful, ripe tomatoes instead of canned ones, and add an extra ½ cup water.

• Add sprigs of fresh oregano or rosemary with the parsley.

• Instead of spinach, use the leaves of 1 or 2 small bunches of arugula or watercress, cut into strips.

• Sprinkle each bowl of soup with about a tablespoon of chopped fresh basil, mint, or chives.

MIDSUMMER VEGETABLE SOUP

MAKES 2 TO 2½ QUARTS

STORAGE
In the refrigerator for 2 to 3 days

◆

1½ cups fresh corn kernels (from 3 plump ears)

1 quart Roasted Vegetable Stock (page 18), Chicken Stock (page 12), or Tarragon Chicken Stock (page 14)

4 ounces sugar snap peas, strings removed, cut into thin slices

1 small red onion, peeled and chopped

1 large red bell pepper, stemmed, cored, and chopped

Chopped raw and cooked seasonal vegetables mixed with stock, lime juice, and hot pepper produce a crunchy texture and fresh summer taste. If you're adding minced jalapeño pepper, do so with restraint. The first time I made the soup I bravely minced one jalapeño, seeds and all, and then recklessly added the remaining ingredients. It was a tossup whether my dinner guests cried with joy and gratitude or simply from the heat of the peppers. The soup should be made at least 4 hours in advance. It's good with corn bread or tostadas.

◆

1 large green bell pepper, stemmed, cored, and chopped
4 or 5 large radishes, trimmed and chopped
1 to 1½ pounds ripe tomatoes (cherry or plum are fine), chopped
1 small ripe avocado, peeled, pitted, and finely cubed
Juice of 1 lime, plus lime juice to taste
Salt
Freshly ground black pepper
2 tablespoons finely chopped fresh basil or coriander
Minced jalapeño pepper (optional)

Place the corn and 1½ cups of stock in a small saucepan, cover and bring to a boil. Cook over moderate heat for 2 minutes. Add the sugar snaps, cover, and cook 1 minute longer. Transfer the mixture to a large bowl and chill.

Add to the corn and sugar snaps the onion, bell peppers, radishes, tomatoes, avocado, juice of 1 lime, remaining stock, salt and pepper to taste, and the chopped basil or coriander. Stir in the jalapeño pepper, if using. Cover the bowl tightly with plastic wrap, or transfer the soup to other containers and cover. Refrigerate for at least 4 hours. Taste for seasoning and add more lime juice to taste. Serve with corn bread, corn chips, or tortilla chips.

V A R I A T I O N S

• If you are adding more chopped vegetables to the soup (instead of substituting comparable amounts), add more stock or water to thin it to a soupy consistency.
• Substitute freshly shelled peas, frozen petits pois, or snow peas for the sugar snaps and cook for 1 minute as you would the sugar snaps.
• Steam 1 small zucchini, trimmed, seeded, and chopped, with the corn and sugar snaps.
• Add chopped peeled and seeded cucumber (perhaps substitute the cucumber for the radishes).
• Use chopped fresh mint instead of basil or coriander.

MINESTRONE

This soup tastes great just off the stove, but even better reheated the next day and the next. It's also delicious served at room temperature sprinkled with a few drops of olive oil and Parmesan.

◆

4 ounces pancetta or salt pork, cut into ¼-inch dice

2 tablespoons olive oil

2 medium onions, peeled and chopped

1 medium leek, trimmed, quartered lengthwise, sliced, and washed

2 to 4 garlic cloves, peeled and minced

2 carrots, peeled and coarsely chopped

2 celery ribs, trimmed and coarsely chopped

8 ounces zucchini, trimmed and cut into ¼-inch dice

4 to 5 ounces green beans, stem ends trimmed and cut into ½-inch lengths

1 pound green or Savoy cabbage, coarsely chopped

1 cup dried cannellini beans, cooked (page 51), with 1 cup cooking liquid reserved

One 28-ounce can imported plum tomatoes, with juices, coarsely chopped

1 quart Brown Beef Stock (page 8), or one 10½-ounce can condensed beef broth plus enough water to equal 1 quart

2 sprigs Italian flat parsley

1 large sprig fresh rosemary

2 or 3 sprigs fresh thyme

Salt

Freshly ground pepper

Generous ½ cup small pasta, preferably imported, such as tubetti or small macaroni

Freshly grated Parmesan cheese

Green Sauce (page 119; optional) or Pesto (page 120; optional)

Combine the pancetta and olive oil in a heavy 5- to 6-quart saucepan and cook over moderate heat, stirring often, until the pancetta has rendered its fat and is crisp. Pancetta and salt pork tend to burn quickly once they've started to brown, so watch carefully. Add the onions, leek, and garlic and sauté for 3 minutes. Add the carrots and celery and sauté 3 minutes longer. Add the zucchini, green beans, and cabbage and cook for 3 minutes, stirring often.

Add the cooked cannellini beans, reserved bean liquid, tomatoes, stock, parsley, rosemary, thyme, and salt and pepper to taste and bring the soup to a boil over moderate heat. Lower the heat, cover the saucepan, and simmer very slowly for 3 hours, stirring from time to time. The minestrone will be very thick.

Turn off the heat and add the pasta, stirring it into the soup. Cover the saucepan and allow the pasta to cook in the heat of the minestrone for about 10 minutes. Serve with a bowl of freshly grated Parmesan, one of the sauces if you like, and crusty Italian bread.

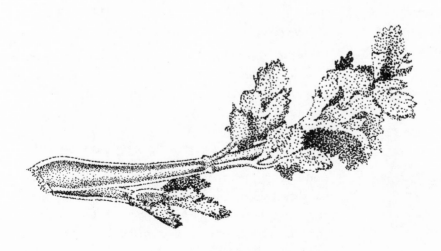

CHILLED BORSCHT

MAKES ABOUT 7 CUPS

A ravishing magenta-colored soup with a rich and slightly tart flavor. The original title for the recipe appears in my handwritten notes as "Copout Borscht," an accurate if inelegant description of the ease with which the soup can be made. Jewish grandmothers and other cooks with rigorous standards will disapprove, but face it, the darn thing works! Freshly made pickled beets from a good deli are best, but even your local supermarket brand of bottled beets are just fine. The garden vegetable variation makes a great summer lunch, and both versions taste better served the next day, especially with a hot, well-seasoned potato sitting in the bowl of pink soup. Pumpernickel or rye bread is de rigueur.

◆

One 16-ounce can cut beets, with juices
1½ cups pickled beets (preferably homemade), drained
1 garlic clove, peeled and minced (optional)
3 cups buttermilk
Fresh lemon juice
Salt
Freshly ground black pepper
For each serving, 1 small new potato in its skin, or 1 small peeled all-purpose potato, cooked until very tender in boiling salted water (optional)
Snipped dill (optional)
Sour cream

Combine the regular canned beets and their juices and the drained pickled beets in the bowl of a food processor fitted with the steel blade. Pulse the beets until they are coarsely chopped; do not chop too fine. Transfer the beets and their juices to a bowl and stir in the garlic, if desired, buttermilk, lemon juice to taste, and salt and pepper, if necessary. Cover the bowl with plastic wrap or pour into a container with a tight lid and refrigerate for about 4 hours.

Ladle the soup into bowls, place a hot boiled potato in each bowl, and sprinkle with dill, if you're using it. Pass a bowl of sour cream separately and serve with pumpernickel or rye bread and butter.

VEGETABLE GARDEN BORSCHT

Add 1½ cups total of diced crisp raw vegetables, such as radishes, celery, peeled and seeded cucumbers, stemmed and seeded red and green bell peppers, zucchini (skin and ¼ inch of flesh only), summer squash, red onion, or scallions, to the finished soup. Chill and serve as directed.

CABBAGE CHOWDER

This is a hearty fall soup, inexpensive and easy to make. I made it first with young white turnips, for which I have a special fondness, and the soup tasted so good I made it again with different combinations of vegetables, including parsnips, tomatoes, and yams. The only constants are the potato soup base, the cabbage, and the milk. Make the soup a day ahead.

◆

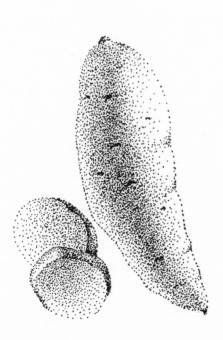

1 recipe Potato Soup Base (page 17), made with 4 ounces lean
    rindless salt pork, diced, in place of butter or oil; 1 clove
    garlic; and thyme
2 carrots, peeled and cut into ¼-inch dice
1 pound green cabbage, cored and shredded or chopped
1 pound parsnips, turnips, pumpkin, winter squash, yams,
    sweet potatoes, green beans, drained canned tomatoes, or a
    combination of vegetables, peeled and seeded if necessary,
    and cut into ⅜-inch dice
Salt
Freshly ground black pepper
2 cups milk, scalded

Place the salt pork in a heavy 4-quart saucepan and render the fat and brown the cracklings over moderately low heat. As the pork begins to brown, watch it carefully and stir often to prevent it from burning. Remove the cracklings with a slotted spoon, drain on paper towels, and reserve. Pour out all but 2 teaspoons of the fat in the pan and proceed with the potato soup base, following the instructions on page 17.

Purée the soup base and return it to the saucepan, add the carrots, cabbage, and diced vegetables, and bring to a boil over high heat. Season with salt and pepper, reduce the heat, and simmer the soup for 15 minutes, partially covered. Add the scalded milk and simmer, uncovered, for 5 minutes. Taste for seasoning again, add the reserved salt pork, and serve with pumpernickel or rye bread.

CREAM OF BROCCOLI SOUP

A recipe based on Leek and Potato Soup (page 92), but with different proportions for the solids and liquids. Here, the leek and onion mixture and the sliced potatoes should measure a generous 2 cups each, but the proportion of liquid is increased. The variation with cheese is especially delicious and makes a substantial dinner, served with bread and followed by a fruit dessert. Serve both soups immediately to best appreciate the fresh taste of broccoli, and the sharp tang of Cheddar in the variation.

◆

1 large leek, white only, trimmed, halved lengthwise, and well washed

1 tablespoon unsalted butter

1 small onion, peeled and chopped

¾ pound potatoes, peeled and sliced

3 cups water

2 sprigs Italian parsley

2 sprigs fresh thyme or a pinch of dried thyme

Salt

Freshly ground black pepper

1½ cups milk, scalded

2 to 2½ cups broccoli florets, steamed until just tender

½ teaspoon soy sauce

Freshly grated nutmeg

Cut the leek halves into ¼-inch-long strips, then into ¼-inch slices. Combine the leek, butter, and onion in a heavy 2-quart saucepan and sauté over moderate heat for 5 minutes; do not allow the leek to brown. Add the potatoes, water, parsley, thyme, and salt and pepper to taste and bring to a boil over high heat. Reduce the heat and simmer the soup, with the cover slightly ajar, for 40 minutes. Add the scalded milk and simmer, uncovered, 10 minutes longer. Taste for seasoning and remove the herb sprigs.

Transfer 1 cup of soup to the bowl of a food processor fitted with the steel blade and pulse 2 or 3 times to make a coarse purée. Add the steamed broccoli and pulse 2 or 3 times more, or until the broccoli is chopped but not puréed. Return the broccoli mixture to the saucepan, add the soy sauce and a small grating of nutmeg, and taste for seasoning. Simmer gently for 2 or 3 minutes. Serve hot at once.

CREAM OF BROCCOLI SOUP WITH CHEDDAR CHEESE

At the end of cooking, stir in 2½ to 4 ounces of grated sharp Cheddar cheese. Cook 2 minutes longer. Serve hot.

CARROT AND PARSNIP SOUP

MAKES 6 CUPS

The flavors of carrots and parsnips play well off each other in this old-fashioned, comforting soup, best made a day ahead.

◆

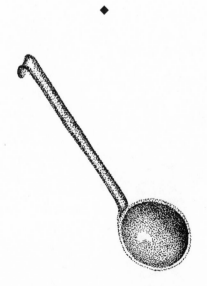

1 tablespoon unsalted butter
1 medium onion, peeled and chopped
1 celery rib, trimmed and cut into ¼-inch dice
12 ounces carrots, peeled and cut into ¼-inch dice
12 ounces parsnips, peeled and cut into ¼-inch dice
1 medium potato (6 ounces), peeled and cut into ¼-inch dice
1 quart Roasted Vegetable Stock (page 18), Chicken Stock (page 12), or one 10½-ounce can condensed chicken broth plus enough water to equal 1 quart
Salt
Freshly ground pepper
2 or 3 sprigs fresh dill
Snipped fresh dill

Combine the butter and onion in a heavy 3-quart saucepan, cover, and place over low heat. Cook for 5 minutes, or until the onion is translucent. Add the celery, carrots, parsnips, potato, stock, salt and pepper to taste, and the sprigs of dill

(continued)

CARROT AND PARSNIP SOUP (*continued*)

and bring to a boil over moderate heat. Cover the pan, lower the heat, and simmer the soup for 20 to 25 minutes, or until the vegetables are soft. Remove and discard the dill sprigs. Serve hot with snipped fresh dill sprinkled over each serving.

CREAMY CARROT AND PARSNIP SOUP

This version has a delicate parsnip flavor. Use the same ingredients, but instead of dicing the celery, carrots, parsnips, and potato, slice them with the medium blade of the food processor. Cook according to directions. When the vegetables are tender, strain them, reserving the broth. Remove the dill sprigs and purée the vegetables in the food processor fitted with the steel blade, adding about ½ cup of the broth while the machine is running. Return the purée to the remaining broth and whisk to blend well. Reheat, if necessary, and serve sprinkled with snipped dill.

Carrot and Sweet Potato Soup with Ginger

Cumin, clove, and fresh ginger add a piquant note to this soup. Serve it hot or cold, with or without the sour cream sauce and chopped coriander. For a somewhat sweeter and more intense flavor, use yams instead of white sweet potatoes.

◆

1 tablespoon vegetable oil

1 medium onion, peeled and chopped

1 or 2 garlic cloves, peeled and minced

12 ounces carrots, peeled and sliced

12 ounces white sweet potatoes, peeled and sliced

5 cups Roasted Vegetable Stock (page 18), Chicken Stock (page 12), or one and a half 10½-ounce cans condensed chicken broth plus enough water to equal 5 cups

1 tablespoon peeled, chopped fresh ginger

1 whole clove

½ teaspoon ground cumin

1 tablespoon finely chopped orange zest

Salt

Freshly ground pepper

½ cup half-and-half

Sour Cream Sauce (page 122; optional)

Chopped fresh coriander or parsley (optional)

Place the vegetable oil, onion, and garlic in a heavy 3-quart saucepan and place over low heat. Cover the pan and sweat the vegetables for 5 minutes. Add the carrots, sweet potatoes, stock, ginger, whole clove, cumin, orange zest, and salt and freshly ground pepper to taste. Cover the pan and bring the soup to a boil. Lower the heat and simmer the mixture for about 20 minutes, or until the vegetables are soft.

Strain the vegetables, reserving the broth. If you can find it, remove the clove from the vegetables and purée them in a food processor fitted with the steel blade, adding ½ cup of the reserved broth as needed.

(continued)

Return the purée and the remaining broth to the saucepan and whisk to blend well. Stir in the half-and-half and bring the soup to a simmer over moderate heat. Cook at a low simmer, uncovered, for 5 minutes. Serve hot or cold with a swirl of sour cream sauce and a sprinkling of chopped coriander, if desired.

CARROT TARRAGON SOUP

MAKES 5 TO 6 CUPS

Tarragon imparts a subtle anise flavor that works very well with carrots, mushrooms, and, of course, in a chicken soup.

◆

1 tablespoon unsalted butter

1 leek, white part only, trimmed, halved lengthwise, thinly sliced, and rinsed in a strainer

2 shallots, peeled and minced

1 garlic clove, peeled and minced

12 ounces carrots, peeled and sliced

5 to 6 ounces potatoes, peeled and sliced

5 cups Tarragon Chicken Stock (page 14), Chicken Stock (page 12), or one and a half 10½-ounce cans condensed chicken broth plus enough water to equal 5 cups

1 large sprig fresh tarragon

1 or 2 sprigs fresh lemon thyme (optional)

1 strip lemon zest

Salt

Freshly ground black pepper
¼ cup half-and-half (optional)
Sour Cream Sauce (page 122) or sour cream
Snipped chives or scallions

In a heavy 3-quart saucepan, melt the butter over low heat. Add the leek, shallots, and garlic, cover the pan, and sweat the vegetables for 5 minutes. Add the carrots, potatoes, stock, tarragon, lemon thyme if using, lemon zest, and salt and pepper to taste and bring the soup to a simmer over high heat. Lower the heat, partially cover the pan, and simmer the soup for 20 minutes.

Strain the solids, reserving the broth. Remove and discard the tarragon and thyme and purée the solids in a food processor until smooth, adding about ½ cup of the reserved liquid as needed. Return the purée to the saucepan, stir in the stock, and taste for seasoning. For a richer flavor, whisk in the half-and-half and simmer for 5 minutes. Serve hot with sour cream sauce and snipped chives.

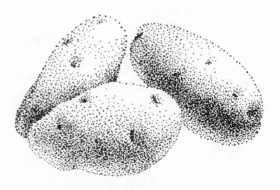

SPICY CAULIFLOWER SOUP

For a vegetarian soup, make the potato soup base with vegetable stock or the cooking liquid from dried white beans. For a spicier flavor, add some of the seeds scraped from the jalapeño pepper.

◆

1 tablespoon vegetable oil

1 garlic clove, peeled and minced

1 medium onion, peeled and chopped

1 jalapeño pepper, stemmed, seeded, and minced

1 large green bell pepper, stemmed, seeded, and coarsely chopped

1 small red bell pepper, stemmed, seeded, and coarsely chopped (optional)

1 teaspoon Madras curry powder, or to taste

1 teaspoon ground cumin, or to taste

1 quart Potato Soup Base (page 17)

1 pound cauliflower florets, steamed until just tender and coarsely chopped

1¾ cups imported canned Italian plum tomatoes, with juices, coarsely chopped

Salt

Freshly ground black pepper

In a heavy 3- to 4-quart saucepan, combine the oil, garlic, onion, and jalapeño and bell peppers, and sauté over moderate heat for about 5 minutes, or until the onions are translucent. Stir in the curry powder and cumin and cook, stirring, for 2 or 3 minutes longer. Add the potato soup base, cauliflower, and tomatoes, season to taste with salt and pepper, and bring to a simmer. Simmer slowly, partially covered, for 10 to 15 minutes, or until the flavors are blended. Serve hot.

CORN CHOWDER

. . . .

MAKES A GENEROUS 2½ QUARTS

Although nothing tastes quite as good as freshly shucked corn, this chowder is a wonderful reminder of summer and its pleasure, even when made with frozen corn kernels. Make this a day in advance so the flavors mature.

◆

2 cups diced unpeeled all-purpose potatoes
1 quart Roasted Vegetable Stock (page 18), Chicken Stock
    (page 12), or one 10½-ounce can condensed chicken broth
    plus enough water to equal 1 quart
1 tablespoon unsalted butter
¼ cup finely chopped lean salt pork
1 garlic clove, peeled and minced
1 large onion, peeled and finely chopped
5 cups corn kernels, cut from fresh corn if possible
1 large tomato, peeled, seeded, and chopped
Salt
Freshly ground black pepper
1 large sprig fresh rosemary
1 large sprig fresh thyme
1 cup milk, scalded
1 cup half-and-half, scalded
1 teaspoon Worcestershire sauce

Place the potatoes and 2 cups of the stock in a 1-quart saucepan and bring to a boil. Cover the pan and boil the potatoes for 8 to 10 minutes, or just until tender. Remove from the heat and set aside.

Place the butter and salt pork in a heavy 3½- to 4-quart saucepan and set over moderately low heat. Cook until the salt pork has rendered most of its fat and the cracklings are browned, stirring often to prevent burning. Remove the salt pork with a slotted spoon, drain on paper towel, and reserve. Add the garlic and onion to the pan and cook, covered, over low heat for about 5 minutes, stirring occasionally.

(continued)

Place 2 cups of the corn kernels and about ½ cup of the remaining stock in a food processor and process until the corn is coarsely puréed. Add to the onion mixture with the remaining 3 cups of whole corn kernels, the remaining stock, the tomato, salt and pepper to taste, and the fresh herbs. Bring to a simmer, cover, and simmer for 8 to 10 minutes.

Scald the milk and half-and-half together and add to the corn mixture along with the cooked potatoes and their liquid. Taste for seasoning and add the Worcestershire sauce. After overnight storage, cook the soup, uncovered, at a slow simmer for 10 minutes. Remove the rosemary and thyme and serve.

TARRAGON-FLAVORED LEEK AND FENNEL SOUP WITH LEMON AND RICE

MAKES 7 CUPS

Tarragon, oregano, chives, mint, and several kinds of thyme run rampant in my garden—not that I'm complaining! The delicate flavor of tarragon, lemon, and olive oil brings out the goodness in the fennel, which is highlighted as well by the fresh taste of anise from the fennel fronds. Don't make the soup unless you have fresh tarragon; the dried herb imparts an insistently bitter flavor. But tarragon chicken

2 tablespoons olive oil

2 shallots or 1 small onion, peeled and minced

2 garlic cloves, peeled and minced

2 large or 3 medium leeks, white only, trimmed, diced, and rinsed

1 large fennel bulb

1½ quarts Tarragon Chicken Stock (page 14), Chicken Stock (page 12), Bean Stock (page 19), or one and a half 10½-ounce cans condensed chicken broth plus enough water to equal 1 quart

stock is not a necessity: Regular chicken stock, bean stock, or canned chicken broth are satisfactory alternatives. A few drops of fruity olive oil and the snipped fennel fronds are all the garnish needed. Serve with a crusty Italian bread.

♦

2 large sprigs fresh tarragon
2 strips lemon zest
Salt
Freshly ground pepper
⅓ cup long-grain or basmati rice
Drops of lemon juice
Freshly grated lemon zest
Drops of olive oil

Combine the olive oil, shallots, and garlic in a heavy 3-quart saucepan and sauté over moderate heat for 2 minutes. Add the leeks and sauté 5 minutes longer.

While the leeks are cooking, prepare the fennel: Cut off the stalks and fronds, reserving the fronds. Quarter the fennel, cut out the core, and chop the bulb into ¼-inch pieces; you should have about 3 cups. Add the chopped fennel to the leek mixture and continue cooking for 5 minutes, stirring occasionally.

Add the stock, tarragon, lemon zest, and salt and pepper to taste and bring the soup to a boil over high heat. Reduce the heat, partially cover the pan, and simmer for 30 minutes. Stir in the rice and cook, covered, for about 12 minutes, or until the rice is almost tender. Turn off the heat and allow the soup to stand, covered, for 15 minutes. The soup can be prepared in advance to this point.

To serve, remove the tarragon sprigs and reheat the soup. Stir in drops of lemon juice and grated lemon zest to taste. Chop the reserved fennel fronds and sprinkle on each serving. Pass a cruet of olive oil.

LEEK AND POTATO SOUP

This is probably my favorite soup. You can double or halve the recipe as long as the same ratio of ingredients is maintained: one part chopped onion and leeks (here it's one generous quart, most of it leeks); one part sliced, peeled potatoes (once again, a generous quart, the slices not too large); one part water; one-half part milk. In the dear dead days beyond recall, before we were able to visualize solid butter lining our arteries, I used to serve this soup with a small piece of golden butter melting serenely on the top.

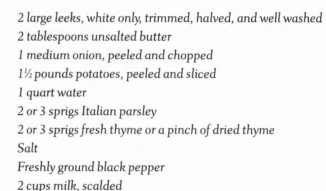

2 large leeks, white only, trimmed, halved, and well washed
2 tablespoons unsalted butter
1 medium onion, peeled and chopped
1½ pounds potatoes, peeled and sliced
1 quart water
2 or 3 sprigs Italian parsley
2 or 3 sprigs fresh thyme or a pinch of dried thyme
Salt
Freshly ground black pepper
2 cups milk, scalded

Cut each leek half into ¼-inch strips, then into ¼-inch slices. Place the leeks, butter, and onion in a heavy 4-quart saucepan and sauté over moderate heat for 5 minutes; do not allow the leeks to brown. Add the potatoes, water, parsley, thyme, and salt and pepper to taste and bring to a boil over high heat. Reduce the heat and simmer the soup, with the cover slightly ajar, for 40 minutes. Add the scalded milk and simmer, uncovered, 10 minutes longer. Taste for seasoning and remove the herb sprigs.

VICHYSSOISE

Cool and then chill 1 recipe of leek and potato soup. Purée the soup in a food processor fitted with the steel blade, adding about 1 cup half-and-half through the feed tube until the mixture is the consistency of heavy cream. Press the vichyssoise through a fine sieve (otherwise the texture will be grainy), taste for seasoning, cover well, and chill again for 30 minutes to allow the flavors to ripen. Serve in chilled soup cups, sprinkled with snipped chives.

CREAMED MUSHROOM SOUP

An old-fashioned soup that's chock full of mushrooms. Slice the mushrooms by hand; they should not be paper-thin. If only large mushrooms are available, cut them into halves, quarters, or thirds before slicing.

◆

2 tablespoons unsalted butter

3 large shallots or 1 medium onion, peeled and minced

1 garlic clove, peeled and minced

1 medium leek, white part only, trimmed, quartered
    lengthwise, sliced, and rinsed

2 pounds small, firm white mushrooms, trimmed and sliced

3 tablespoons flour

3½ to 4 cups Roasted Vegetable Stock (page 18), Chicken
    Stock (page 12), or one 10½-ounce can condensed chicken
    broth plus enough water to equal 1 quart

2 sprigs fresh thyme or rosemary or ¼ teaspoon dried thyme

1 bay leaf

1 strip lemon zest

Salt

Freshly ground black pepper

1 cup milk, scalded

1 cup half-and-half, scalded

Drops of soy sauce

Place the butter, shallots, garlic, and leek in a heavy 3-quart saucepan and sauté over moderate heat for about 5 minutes, or until the shallots are translucent. Add the mushrooms and cook over high heat, stirring often, until the mushroom liquid has evaporated, about 10 minutes.

Sprinkle the flour over the mushrooms and cook, stirring constantly, over moderate heat for about 3 minutes. Add the stock, thyme, bay leaf, lemon zest, and salt and pepper to taste and bring to a boil. Lower the heat and simmer the soup, uncovered, for 15 minutes. Add the scalded milk and half-and-half and cook at a very low simmer for about 5 minutes. Stir in the soy sauce and taste for seasoning. Remove the fresh herb, bay leaf, and lemon zest, and serve hot.

DOUBLE MUSHROOM SOUP

The intense, earthy flavor of this soup depends wholly on the quality of your dried mushrooms. Use only the best imported porcini or morels. Although the soup is expensive, it is so rich that small servings suffice. It is especially good with pumpernickel.

◆

1¾ ounces imported dried mushrooms, preferably porcini or morels
2½ cups water
2 tablespoons unsalted butter
2 large shallots, peeled and chopped
1½ pounds champignon mushrooms, rinsed (if necessary) and finely chopped
Juice of 1 lemon
2 cups Chicken Stock (page 12)
1 bay leaf
2 or 3 sprigs fresh thyme or a pinch of dried thyme
2 or 3 sprigs fresh dill
Salt
Freshly ground pepper
2 cups heavy cream, scalded
Freshly grated nutmeg (optional)
Sour cream
Snipped fresh dill

Combine the dried mushrooms and the water in a small saucepan and bring to a simmer. Cover the pan, remove from the heat, and let the mushrooms soak for 20 minutes. Transfer the mushrooms to a strainer and place them under running water to rinse out any residue of sand. Drain the mushrooms, dry them on paper towels, and chop coarsely. Reserve. Pour the mushroom soaking liquid through a strainer lined with a paper towel. Reserve.

Combine the butter and shallots in a heavy 3-quart saucepan and sauté over moderate heat for about 5 minutes, or until the shallots are translucent. Add the champignon mushrooms and lemon juice and cook over high heat, stirring often, until the juice and mushroom liquid have evaporated, about 10 minutes. Add the reserved dried mushrooms, their strained soaking liquid, the stock, bay leaf, thyme, dill, and salt and pepper to taste and bring to a boil. Lower the heat and simmer the soup, uncovered, for 15 minutes. Add the scalded cream and cook at a very low simmer for about 5 minutes. Stir in the nutmeg if you are using it and taste for seasoning. Remove the bay leaf and fresh herbs and serve hot, garnishing each portion with a dollop of sour cream sprinkled with snipped dill.

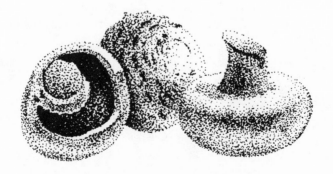

FRENCH ONION SOUP

* *

MAKES 7 CUPS

The key to a rich onion soup is the slow, even browning of the onions, which takes a good 35 minutes. It's tempting to raise the heat to hasten the process. Don't do it: The onions will brown faster, but they'll be undercooked. If you find it maddening to stand around watching the pot while the onions take their own sweet time to brown, you can always undertake another recipe or a kitchen chore that will allow you enough time to reach over and stir the onions now and then.

◆

3 tablespoons unsalted butter

1 tablespoon vegetable oil

1½ to 2 pounds yellow onions, peeled and sliced

Small pinch of sugar

4 teaspoons flour

¼ cup red wine

2 quarts Brown Beef Stock (page 8), or two 10½-ounce cans condensed beef broth plus enough water to equal 2 quarts

2 sprigs fresh thyme

2 sprigs Italian parsley

Salt

Freshly ground pepper

Combine the butter, oil, and onions in a heavy 3½- to 4-quart saucepan and cook over moderately low heat for about 35 minutes, tossing to cover the onions with fat and stirring often, until the onions are completely golden brown, very soft, and slightly caramelized. Sprinkle the sugar over the onions during the last 10 minutes of cooking to speed up the caramelization process.

Sprinkle the flour over the onions and cook 3 or 4 minutes, stirring often. Do not allow the mixture to burn. Add the red wine and ½ cup of the stock and cook over high heat for a few minutes, until the liquid is almost completely reduced. Stir in the remaining stock, the thyme, parsley, and salt and pepper to taste. Bring the soup to a boil, reduce the heat, and simmer, uncovered, for about 45 minutes. Remove the herb sprigs, taste for seasoning, and serve very hot, with Parmesan toasts if you like.

ROASTED ONION AND POTATO SOUP

Roasted onions and potatoes are a no-work accompaniment to roasts, chops, omelets, and other main courses. In this soup, their rich flavor is intensified by simmering them in beef stock with rosemary. For a thick, chunky soup, slice the onions and potatoes no thinner than ⅛ inch thick. Serve with crusty bread.

◆

1½ pounds onions, peeled, quartered, and sliced

2 pounds potatoes, washed, quartered lengthwise, and sliced

7 to 10 garlic cloves (or to taste), lightly crushed with the flat of a knife and peeled

3 to 4 tablespoons olive oil or unsalted butter, melted

Salt

Freshly ground black pepper

6 cups Brown Beef Stock (page 8), or one and a half 10½-ounce cans concentrated beef broth plus enough water to equal 6 cups

1 tablespoon balsamic vinegar, plus vinegar to taste

1 sprig fresh rosemary

1 tablespoon Madeira (optional)

Preheat the oven to 450° F.

Place the onions, potatoes, garlic, olive oil, and salt and pepper to taste in a large shallow flameproof roasting pan and toss with your hands until the vegetables are well coated with the oil. Spread out the vegetables and bake in the bottom third of the oven for 10 minutes. Stir the vegetables with a spatula, spread them out again, and roast 10 minutes longer. Reduce the oven temperature to 375° F. and roast the vegetables for 45 minutes, stirring and scraping them from the bottom with the spatula every 15 minutes.

Scrape the roasted vegetables into a heavy 3- to 4-quart saucepan. Place the roasting pan over moderate direct heat, add ½ cup of the stock and the balsamic vinegar, and deglaze the pan, stirring and scraping the caramelized bits of

(continued)

potatoes and onion from the bottom and sides of the pan. Reduce the deglazing liquid slightly, then scrape it into the saucepan of vegetables.

Add to the vegetables the remaining 5½ cups of stock and the rosemary and taste for seasoning. Bring to a simmer, cover the pan, and cook slowly for about 45 minutes, adding water as necessary to thin the soup. Taste for seasoning again, and add the Madeira or an additional teaspoon or two of balsamic vinegar. Allow the soup to cool for about 5 minutes, remove the rosemary sprig, then serve.

ROASTED ONION AND POTATO SOUP WITH WILD MUSHROOMS

MAKES 7 ½ TO 8 CUPS

This is a deluxe version of the preceding soup.

1½ pounds onions, peeled, quartered, and sliced

2 pounds potatoes, washed, quartered lengthwise, and sliced

7 to 10 garlic cloves (or to taste), lightly crushed with the flat of a knife and peeled

3 to 4 tablespoons unsalted butter, melted

Salt

Freshly ground black pepper

¾ ounce imported dried porcini mushrooms

1½ cups hot water

1 quart Brown Beef Stock (page 8), or one 10½-ounce can concentrated beef broth plus enough water to equal 1 quart

1 tablespoon balsamic vinegar

1 sprig fresh rosemary
1 to 2 teaspoons paprika, or to taste
1⅓ cups half-and-half, scalded
1 teaspoon soy sauce, or to taste

Preheat the oven to 450° F.

Follow the instructions on page 97 for roasting the onions, potatoes, and garlic. While they are roasting, soak the dried porcini mushrooms in the hot water in a small bowl for about 20 minutes. Remove the mushrooms from the water, squeezing the soaking liquid back into the bowl. Place the mushrooms in a strainer and rinse briefly to remove any sand left in them. Chop the mushrooms and reserve. Pour the soaking liquid through a strainer lined with a paper towel, set aside ½ cup, and add the remaining liquid to the stock.

Scrape the roasted vegetables into a heavy 3- to 4-quart saucepan. Place the roasting pan over moderate direct heat, add the ½ cup of mushroom liquid and the balsamic vinegar, and deglaze the pan, stirring and scraping the caramelized bits of potatoes and onion from the bottom and sides of the pan. Reduce the deglazing liquid slightly, then scrape it into the saucepan of vegetables.

Add the stock, rosemary, paprika, and chopped mushrooms and taste for seasoning. Bring to a simmer, cover the pan, and cook slowly for about 45 minutes, adding water as necessary to thin the soup. Stir in the scalded half-and-half and simmer, uncovered, 10 minutes longer. Add the soy sauce and taste for seasoning. Remove the rosemary sprig and allow the soup to cool for about 5 minutes before serving.

CREAMED PEAR AND ONION SOUP WITH GINGER AND LEMON

MAKES 7 TO 7½ CUPS

This refreshing and elegant soup is most appealing served cold the day after it is made. For a light summer lunch, add an accompaniment of toasted French or Italian bread with Gorgonzola or Roquefort cheese and follow with a tossed salad.

When you grate the ginger, the idea is to get the flavorful essence of the root but not the fibrous matter. I simply grate it through the medium-fine holes of a hand-held grater, and the result is a coarse paste.

The flavor of the soup needs no enhancement, but its color is an uncompromising beige, so a garnish of some kind is called for. The simplest is a sprinkling of chopped chives or parsley, the most sinful a dollop of lightly salted whipped cream strewn with chopped almonds.

◆

3 ripe pears (about 1¼ pounds), peeled, stemmed, cored, and cut into small chunks
2 medium onions, peeled and thinly sliced
1 quart Brown Beef Stock (page 8), or one 10½-ounce can condensed beef broth plus enough water to equal 1 quart
2-inch piece of fresh ginger, peeled and grated through the medium-fine holes of a hand grater (about 2 teaspoons grated ginger)
Grated rind of 1 large lemon
2 cups half-and-half
Salt
Freshly ground white pepper
2 teaspoons rum (optional)

GARNISHES
Chopped toasted sliced natural almonds; unblanched almonds, chopped quite fine, but not ground; finely snipped chives or young scallion greens; finely chopped Italian parsley; a dollop of lightly salted whipped cream; or Sour Cream Sauce (page 122).

Place the pears, onions, and beef broth in a 3- to 4-quart heavy-bottomed saucepan and bring to a slow simmer over moderate heat. Reduce the heat and simmer, partially covered, for about 40 minutes, or until the pears and onions are very soft. The soup can be prepared in advance to this stage and stored, tightly covered, in the refrigerator or freezer.

Add the ginger, grated lemon zest, half-and-half, and salt and pepper to taste. Heat the mixture until it is barely simmering and cook, partially covered, over very low heat for 10 to 15 minutes. Stir in the rum, if desired, and cook a few minutes longer. Transfer the mixture in batches to a blender or a food processor fitted with the steel blade and purée. (The blender will produce a silkier texture.) Serve hot or cold with one of the garnishes.

CREAMED APPLE AND ONION SOUP WITH GINGER AND LEMON

Use about 1¼ pounds of sweet apples, such as McIntosh or Paula, instead of the pears. For a smoother texture, peel the apples as well as stemming and coring them. Substitute applejack or Calvados for the rum.

CHILLED ROASTED PEPPER SOUP WITH BUTTERMILK

. . . .

MAKES 4 TO 5 CUPS

Red peppers, oven-roasted in a shallow pan with garlic and olive oil, are themselves a delicious appetizer or side dish, a welcome addition to the buffet table, and not bad over pasta. Cooked and puréed with stock and then combined with buttermilk, the peppers are transformed into a gorgeous red soup subtly flavored with garlic and cumin. Red peppers are most abundant in late summer, which is a good time to serve this superb soup.

◆

1½ to 2 pounds red bell peppers, stemmed, seeded, membranes removed, and cut into eighths

2 jalapeño peppers, stemmed, seeded, and cut into quarters (optional)

10 garlic cloves, lightly crushed with the flat of a knife and peeled

2 tablespoons olive oil

1 quart Roasted Vegetable Stock (page 18), Chicken Stock (page 12), or one 10½-ounce can condensed chicken broth plus enough water to equal 1 quart

1 tablespoon balsamic vinegar

1 or 2 sprigs fresh oregano

Pinch of ground cumin

Salt

Freshly ground pepper

1½ cups buttermilk

Chopped fresh chives or coriander

Preheat the oven to 450° F.

Combine the bell peppers, jalapeño peppers if desired, garlic, and olive oil in a 9 x 13-inch flameproof roasting pan and toss to coat the vegetables evenly with the oil. Bake for 10 minutes, stir the peppers, and reduce the oven temperature to 350° F. Continue to roast the peppers and garlic 45 to 50 minutes longer, or until they are soft and lightly caramelized, stirring every 15 minutes. Transfer the peppers and garlic to a 2- to 3-quart saucepan. Place the roasting pan over a stove-top burner set to moderate heat and deglaze the pan with ½ cup of the stock and the balsamic vinegar, scraping up all the caramelized vegetables from the bottom and sides of the pan. Reduce the deglazing liquid to about ⅓ cup and add it to the saucepan with the remaining stock, oregano, ground cumin, and salt and pepper to taste. Bring the soup to a slow simmer and cook, uncovered, for 25 to 30 minutes.

Purée the soup in a food processor fitted with the steel blade, then force the purée through a fine sieve; there should be about 3 cups of purée. Taste for seasoning. The soup can be prepared ahead to this point and either chilled or frozen. To finish the soup, stir in the buttermilk, taste for seasoning again, and chill for at least 4 hours, or preferably overnight. Sprinkle the soup with snipped chives or chopped coriander and serve in chilled cups.

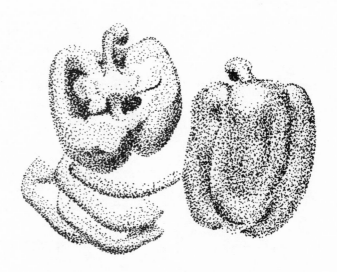

CURRIED ACORN SQUASH SOUP

MAKES ABOUT 2 QUARTS

This is a lovely soup for autumn, with its silken texture, spirited taste, and golden orange color reminiscent of the harvest moon.

◆

2½ to 3 pounds acorn squash
1 tablespoon vegetable oil
2 medium onions, peeled and chopped
1 large Granny Smith apple, cored and coarsely chopped
3 tablespoons chopped fresh ginger
2½ to 3 teaspoons curry powder
2 to 3 teaspoons ground cumin
¾ teaspoon ground cardamom
5½ cups Chicken Stock (page 12)
¾ cup half-and-half
1½ tablespoons dark brown sugar (optional)
Salt
Freshly ground white pepper
Hulled pumpkin seeds

Preheat the oven to 375° F.

Pierce the acorn squash in several places with a long 2-tined fork, place on a foil-lined baking sheet, and roast for about 1 hour, or until the squash is very tender. Remove from the oven and allow to cool. Halve and seed the squash, then scoop out the soft flesh and reserve it; you should have about 3 cups.

Heat the oil in a heavy 4- to 5-quart saucepan over moderately low heat, add the onions, and sauté slowly until they are translucent, about 5 minutes. Add the chopped apple and ginger and sauté the mixture for 5 minutes. Stir in the curry powder, cumin, and cardamom and continue to cook for about 5 minutes, stirring often. Add the chicken stock and slowly bring to a boil. Add the reserved squash to the soup mixture and bring to a boil. Lower the heat and simmer the soup, covered, for about 1 hour.

Strain the solids, reserving the liquid in a large bowl. Purée the solids in batches in a food processor fitted with the steel blade and stir the purée into the liquid. Pass the soup through a sieve placed over the original saucepan, pressing on the fibrous ginger and squash to extract all the liquid. Add the half-and-half, brown sugar if desired, and salt and pepper to taste, and heat. Serve the soup hot, but not boiling.

To toast the pumpkin seeds, preheat the oven to 350° F. Spread the seeds on a baking sheet and bake them for about 15 minutes, or until they are somewhat browned and crisp. Sprinkle the seeds over the soup just before serving, or put them in a bowl and pass them around separately.

CREAMED SPINACH AND MUSHROOM SOUP

The mushroom soup and the chopped cooked spinach can be prepared well ahead of time, even a day in advance, and combined just before serving. Although the soup tastes passable made with frozen chopped spinach, fresh spinach gives it real distinction. If possible, use bunches of spinach, not the bagged variety. You'll have to trim and wash it more vigilantly, but the gain in quality is worth the extra effort.

◆

1 recipe Creamed Mushroom Soup (page 93)
2 teaspoons unsalted butter
10 ounces fresh spinach leaves, very thoroughly washed and
    drained
Salt
Freshly ground black pepper
Freshly grated nutmeg

Prepare the mushroom soup as directed. In a large skillet (preferably nonstick), melt the butter over moderate heat, add the spinach, and cook, stirring often, until the spinach is barely cooked, about 4 minutes.

Using tongs or a slotted spoon, transfer the spinach to a sieve held over the skillet. Press on the spinach to drain as much liquid as possible back into the skillet. Reduce the juices in the skillet to about ¼ cup.

Meanwhile, place the spinach on a cutting board and chop coarsely. Add the spinach and its reduced cooking liquid to the finished soup and bring to a simmer over moderate heat. Adjust the seasoning, and add nutmeg to taste. Cook at a simmer, uncovered, for about 5 minutes, or until the flavors are blended. Do not overcook the spinach, and serve as soon as it is tender.

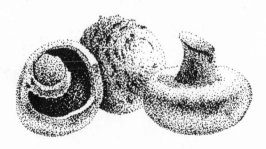

ORANGE SQUASH SOUP

This delicate soup requires a full-bodied stock to bring out the flavor of the squash.

◆

2 teaspoons unsalted butter or vegetable oil

1 medium onion, peeled, quartered, and thinly sliced

One 1½- to 2-pound winter squash (Hubbard, butternut), peeled, seeds removed, and cut into ½-inch pieces

2 carrots, peeled and sliced

6 cups Roasted Vegetable Stock (page 18), Chicken Stock (page 12), or one and a half 10½-ounce cans condensed chicken broth plus enough water to equal 6 cups

1 tablespoon dark brown sugar

½ teaspoon ground cardamom

1 large sprig fresh thyme

1 long strip orange zest

Salt

½ cup fresh orange juice

2 tablespoons Grand Marnier or dark rum (optional)

Sour Cream Sauce (page 122) or sour cream

Combine the butter and onion in a heavy 4-quart saucepan over moderately low heat and sauté slowly for 5 minutes, or until the onion is translucent. Add the squash, carrots, stock, brown sugar, cardamom, thyme, orange zest, and salt to taste. Partially cover the pan and bring the soup to a boil. Lower the heat and simmer, partially covered, until the carrots and squash are tender, about 30 minutes.

Remove and discard the thyme and orange zest, then transfer the soup to a food processor fitted with the steel blade and purée. Return the soup to the saucepan, add the orange juice and the Grand Marnier, if desired, taste for seasoning, and reheat. Serve with sour cream sauce or plain sour cream.

CHUNKY TOMATO SOUP

An old favorite, just like mom used to make. It's delicious with Parmesan or mozzarella toast and a salad.

◆

4 ounces rindless salt pork, cut into ¼-inch dice

2 or 3 garlic cloves, peeled and minced

2 medium onions, peeled and chopped

2 celery ribs, trimmed, halved or quartered lengthwise, and sliced

2 tablespoons flour

2 medium potatoes, peeled and cubed to make 2½ to 3 cups

One 28-ounce can imported Italian plum tomatoes, with the juice, coarsely chopped

3 cups Roasted Vegetable Stock (page 18), Bean Stock (page 19), Chicken Stock (page 12), or half a 10½-ounce can condensed chicken broth plus enough water to equal 3 cups

1 bay leaf

A pinch of ground cloves

Salt

Freshly ground black pepper

1 to 1½ cups mixed fresh or frozen vegetables (zucchini, yellow squash, carrots, green peas, green beans, lima beans, corn), cut into small pieces, if necessary

2 cups milk, scalded

In a heavy 4-quart saucepan, render the salt pork over moderate heat. Lower the heat as the pork begins to brown and watch to see that it does not burn. With a slotted spoon, transfer the pork to a double layer of paper towels.

Pour out all but 2 tablespoons of fat from the pan and add the garlic and onions. Sauté over moderate heat for 4 minutes, then add the celery and sauté 4 minutes longer. Stir in the flour and cook, stirring constantly, for 2 minutes. Add the potatoes, plum tomatoes and their juice, stock, bay leaf, ground cloves, and salt and pepper to taste. Bring to a boil over high heat, reduce the heat, partially cover the pan, and simmer the soup for 20 minutes.

Add the vegetables and simmer, partially covered, 20 minutes longer, or until all the vegetables are tender. Stir in the scalded milk and taste for seasoning. Simmer for 10 minutes, remove the bay leaf, and serve.

CHILLED GINGERED TOMATO SOUP
WITH GARDEN VEGETABLES

. . . .

MAKES 5 CUPS

Ginger and buttermilk give a tangy lift to canned tomatoes. The tomato-buttermilk mixture can be served without the vegetables as a smooth soup or a refreshing drink.

◆

1 tablespoon vegetable oil

2 or 3 garlic cloves, peeled and minced

1 medium onion, peeled and chopped

1 walnut-size nugget fresh ginger, peeled and minced

One 28-ounce can Italian plum tomatoes, with their juices, coarsely chopped

2 cups Roasted Vegetable Stock (page 18), Chicken Stock (page 12), or half a 10½-ounce can concentrated chicken broth plus enough water to equal 2 cups

1 pinch ground cloves

1 strip lemon zest

1 small bay leaf

Salt

Freshly ground black pepper

Drops of lemon juice

1 cup buttermilk

1 to 1½ cups mixed diced raw vegetables (radishes, peeled and seeded cucumber, celery, carrots, zucchini, scallions, red or Spanish onion, and green bell pepper)

Chopped fresh basil or coriander

Combine the oil, garlic, onion, and ginger in a heavy 2-quart saucepan and sauté the vegetables over moderate heat for 5 minutes. Add the tomatoes, stock, cloves, lemon zest, bay leaf, and salt and pepper to taste and bring the soup to a simmer. Reduce the heat, partially cover the pan, and simmer the soup for 15 to 20 minutes.

Transfer the soup to a food processor fitted with the steel blade and purée. Force the purée through a fine strainer into a bowl and add the lemon juice, buttermilk, and diced vegetables. Taste for seasoning, cover, and chill. Serve cold with chopped basil or coriander. Garlic bread is a good accompaniment, as are breadsticks.

YAM AND WINTER SQUASH SOUP

MAKES A GENEROUS 2½ QUARTS

STORAGE
In the refrigerator for 2 to 3 days;
frozen for up to 2 months

Because the yams and squash all
bake together on a foil-lined
baking sheet, this is an
exceptionally easy soup. To get as
much as possible out of 1½ hours
of baking time, I make it in
quantity and freeze leftovers.
However, if your storage space is
limited, you can halve the recipe.
The soup tastes best when made
with the yams and at least two
different kinds of squash.

◆

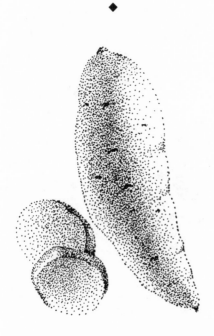

1 medium acorn squash (about 1½ pounds)
1 dumpling or Hubbard squash (about 2 pounds)
4 medium yams (about 2 pounds), scrubbed
1 large Spanish onion, unpeeled
Vegetable oil
6½ cups Roasted Vegetable Stock (page 18), Chicken Stock
    (page 12), or one and a half 10½-ounce cans condensed
    chicken broth plus enough water to equal 6½ cups
2 teaspoons soy sauce
1 teaspoon grated orange zest
Salt
Freshly ground white or black pepper
1 cup half-and-half or heavy cream
Freshly grated nutmeg

Preheat the oven to 375° F. Line a baking sheet or jelly roll
pan with foil.

Prick the acorn and other squash in several places with a
2-tined fork. Rub the squash, yams, and onion lightly with
vegetable oil and arrange them on the baking sheet. Bake
the vegetables for 1½ hours, or until they are very tender and
somewhat caramelized. Remove the pan from the oven and
allow the vegetables to cool.

Cut the squash in half and scoop out the seeds. Scoop the
flesh into a bowl. Peel the yams and add to the bowl. Peel
the onion, trim off the root end, and add to the bowl. In a
food processor fitted with the steel blade, purée the
vegetables in batches, adding about 4 cups of the stock to
facilitate the process.

Transfer the purée to a heavy 4-quart saucepan, add the remaining stock, soy sauce, grated orange zest, and salt and pepper to taste. Bring the soup to a simmer, and cook, partially covered, for 15 minutes. Stir in the half-and-half and taste for seasoning. Simmer the soup, uncovered, 5 minutes longer. Serve sprinkled with nutmeg.

PURÉED VEGETABLE SOUPS

Fresh vegetables, sliced or cut into manageable pieces, can be cooked quickly in a small amount of water and stock with herbs and a few seasonings and then puréed in the food processor, producing a thick, porridgelike soup. Serve it at once with drops of olive oil and Parmesan cheese or with sour cream or green sauce or pesto. Because the preparation is so simple, the quality of the vegetables is crucial to the flavor and to the nutritional value as well.

The vegetable combinations are endless, with lots of room to experiment, depending on your food preferences and what's available at the market. You'll soon discover the properties of various vegetables, which ones become fibrous when they're puréed, which flavors dominate, and what proportion of vegetables to liquid tastes best to you. Note that these purées should be served at once, not stored or frozen.

To get you started, here are a few combinations that have worked for me.

Purée of Potatoes and Broccoli

MAKES A GENEROUS 6 CUPS

1 large onion, peeled and cut into cubes
2 to 4 large garlic cloves, crushed with the flat of a knife and peeled
1 large leek, trimmed, halved lengthwise, sliced and rinsed
2 or 3 carrots, peeled and sliced
9 ounces red potatoes, unpeeled, cut into cubes
2¼ cups water
2¼ cups Roasted Vegetable Stock (page 18), Chicken Stock (page 12), or half a 10½-ounce can condensed chicken broth plus enough water to equal 2¼ cups
Florets from 1 large bunch broccoli
Salt
Freshly ground pepper

Place the onion, garlic, leek, carrots, potatoes, water, and stock in a heavy 3- to 4-quart saucepan and bring to a boil over high heat. Cover the pan, lower the heat, and cook the soup at a slow boil for 15 minutes. Add the broccoli florets, cover the pan, and return to a slow boil. Cook for 7 to 10 minutes, or just until the broccoli is tender. Add salt and pepper.

Transfer the soup to the bowl of a food processor fitted with the steel blade and purée, in batches if necessary. You can leave a few lumps in the soup if you like—flecks of carrot look quite pretty. Taste for seasoning and serve soon, very warm but not boiling hot, accompanied by cheese toasts or toasted cheese bread.

PURÉE OF YAMS, CARROTS, TURNIPS, AND APPLE

MAKES 7 CUPS

This was more a spontaneous "icebox" soup than a planned recipe. Aside from the standard vegetables—carrots, leek, onion, garlic, celery—I happened to have on hand 2 turnips, the apple, yams, and some kale, which had not found its way into another soup I'd planned. Delicious.

◆

1 medium onion, peeled and sliced

1 small leek, white only, halved, sliced, and rinsed

2 garlic cloves, peeled and halved

2 celery ribs, trimmed and sliced

3 or 4 carrots, peeled and sliced

2 medium turnips, peeled and sliced

10 ounces yams, peeled and sliced

1 medium apple, stemmed, cored, and sliced

3 cups shredded kale leaves

3 fresh sage leaves

2 sprigs Italian parsley

1 cup water

1 cup Roasted Vegetable Stock (page 18), Chicken Stock (page 12), or ¼ cup condensed chicken broth plus ¾ cup water

Pinch ground cloves

Salt

Freshly ground pepper

Combine all the ingredients in a heavy 4-quart saucepan and bring to a boil over high heat. Reduce the heat, cover the pan, and simmer the vegetables until the yams and turnips are tender, 15 to 20 minutes. Purée the soup in batches in a food processor fitted with the steel blade and reheat, if necessary. Serve at once with sour cream or plain yogurt.

Purée of Fennel, Carrots, and Leek

1 medium onion, peeled and quartered

1 large bulb fennel, trimmed, with some of the fronds reserved
    (especially the very young fronds), cut into ½-inch cubes

12 ounces carrots, trimmed, peeled, and cut into 1-inch pieces

1 leek, white only, sliced, washed well, and drained

2 strips orange zest

2 allspice berries

2 cups water

2 cups Roasted Vegetable Stock (page 18), Chicken Stock
    (page 12), or half a 10½-ounce can condensed chicken
    broth plus enough water to equal 2 cups

½ bunch fresh dill, rinsed and drained

1 tablespoon fruity olive oil

Salt

Place the onion, fennel, carrots, leek, orange zest, allspice
berries, water, and stock in a heavy 4- to 5-quart pot, cover,
and bring to a boil over high heat. Reduce the heat and cook
the soup at a medium-fast boil for 18 minutes, or until the
vegetables are soft. Add the reserved fennel fronds and dill,
cover, and cook about 4 minutes, or until the greens are very
limp but still quite green. If the liquid has not reduced to 2
to 2½ cups, remove the lid and boil for a few minutes more.
Remove the allspice berries (if you can find them) and purée
the soup in a food processor fitted with a steel blade. With
the motor running, add the olive oil and some salt and
process until it is emulsified. Taste for seasoning and serve
at once.

SAUCES

The following sauce recipes can all be mixed up a day or two ahead of time and refrigerated. As you experiment with soup garnishes, you will doubtless think of other sauces that would be equally tasty additions. Look for compatibility of flavor, but contrast in color—a pretty dollop of vivid green on a pale green surface, or of pink on a creamy beige soup.

GREEN SAUCE

For an even snappier sauce, add 1 or 2 drained anchovies or a tablespoon of drained capers with the garlic and lemon juice. If you have fresh herbs in your garden, by all means include a few leaves of one congenial with the soup this is to garnish.

◆

1 cup roughly chopped parsley leaves
1 scallion, both white and green parts, sliced
¼ cup chopped fresh spinach or watercress leaves
½ teaspoon chopped garlic
2 tablespoons freshly squeezed lemon juice
½ to ¾ cup olive oil
Salt and freshly ground black pepper

In a food processor fitted with the steel blade, mince the parsley, scallion, and spinach or watercress. Add the garlic and lemon juice and process to blend. With the motor running, add the olive oil in a thin stream to make a thick sauce. Season to taste and refrigerate.

PESTO

Pesto recipes abound, but if you haven't a favorite, do try this one. Its beautiful green color is best preserved by filming the finished sauce with olive oil before storing it, covered, in the refrigerator.

◆

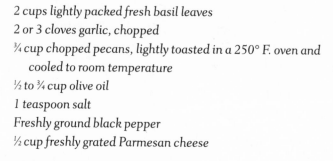

2 cups lightly packed fresh basil leaves
2 or 3 cloves garlic, chopped
¾ cup chopped pecans, lightly toasted in a 250° F. oven and cooled to room temperature
½ to ¾ cup olive oil
1 teaspoon salt
Freshly ground black pepper
½ cup freshly grated Parmesan cheese

Place the basil, garlic, and toasted nuts in a food processor fitted with the steel blade and process until finely minced. With the motor running, drizzle in the olive oil to make a paste that is not too liquid. (You may have to stop and push basil leaves down into the mixture with a rubber spatula.) Remove the pesto from the processor to a bowl and stir in the salt, pepper, and Parmesan.

ROUILLE

MAKES ABOUT ¾ CUP

This is the traditional Provençal sauce for fish soups and stews. If you and your friends have asbestos palates, be generous with the Tabasco or add some hot pepper flakes with the garlic.

◆

1 red bell pepper, roasted, peeled, seeded, and roughly chopped
2 cloves garlic, peeled and chopped
1 slice good-quality white bread, torn into pieces
Drops of Tabasco sauce, to taste
½ teaspoon salt
Freshly ground pepper
¼ to ½ cup olive oil
Drops of freshly squeezed lemon juice (optional)

Place the red pepper, garlic, torn bread, Tabasco, and salt and pepper in a blender or food processor fitted with the steel blade and purée. With the motor running, add the olive oil a few drops at a time until the sauce is thick, like a mayonnaise. Remove to a bowl and check the seasoning. Cover and store in the refrigerator. Thin at serving time with lemon juice if you like.

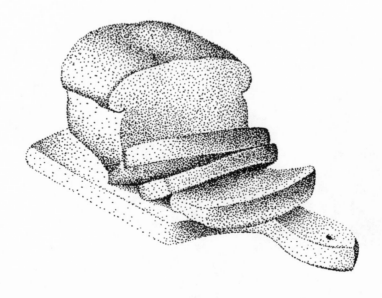

SOUR CREAM SAUCE

A lovely multipurpose sauce that goes well with cold seafood, chilled vegetables, and hard-boiled eggs, and swirls handsomely into various soups.

◆

1 tablespoon Dijon, Champagne, or other superior prepared mustard
1 tablespoon Worcestershire sauce
1 tablespoon grated horseradish
Salt and freshly ground black pepper
1 cup commercial sour cream
Minced fresh dill, or tiny leaves of fresh oregano or thyme

In a bowl blend the mustard, Worcestershire, horseradish, and salt and pepper. Stir in the sour cream thoroughly, and then fold in the herb of your choice. Correct the seasoning and refrigerate the sauce.

INDEX

corn, 89–90
shrimp and scallop
(variation), 31
Chunky tomato soup, 108–109
Clam:
chowder I, 26–27
chowder II, 28–29
Clam juice, as fish stock
substitute, 5, 15
Classic split pea soup, 68
Corn chowder, 89–90
Cream of broccoli soup, 82
with cheddar cheese
(variation), 83
Creamed apple and onion soup
with ginger and lemon
(variation), 101
Creamed mushroom soup, 93
Creamed pear and onion soup
with ginger and
lemon, 100–101
Creamed spinach and
mushroom soup, 106
Creamy carrot and parsnip
soup (variation), 84
Curried acorn squash soup,
104–105
Curried cream of chicken soup
with apples and
onions, 46
Curried split pea soup, 69

D

Double mushroom soup, 94–95

E

Eggplant, in ratatouille soup
with meatballs, 36–38

F

Fennel:
carrots, and leek, purée of,
116

and leek soup with lemon
and rice, tarragon-
flavored, 90–91
Fish:
soup, Barbara's (cotriade),
24
stock, 15
substitute for, 5, 15
tomato, 16
see also Shellfish
Fish soups:
about, 21
Barbara's (cotriade), 24
clam chowder I, 26–27
clam chowder II, 28–29
mussel, 23
shellfish (variation), 25
shrimp, with saffron and
tomatoes, 30–31
shrimp and scallop
chowder (variation),
31
French onion soup, 96

G

Garlic and cannellini bean
soup, 58–59
Garnishes. *See* Sauces
Ginger:
carrot and sweet potato
soup with, 85–86
grating, 100
and lemon, creamed pear
and onion soup with,
100–101
tomato soup with garden
vegetables, chilled,
110–11
Gray, Ruth, 36
Green sauce, 119
Greens:
chick-pea and sausage soup
with, 60
lentil, yam, and tomato soup
with, 62–64

ABOUT THE AUTHOR

. . . .

JUDY KNIPE is an artist and cookbook writer and editor. She is the coauthor, with
Edward J. Safdie, of *Spa Food* and *New Spa Food*, and with Barbara Marks,
of *The Christmas Cookie Book*. She divides her time between
New York City and Vermont.